500

Tips for

Primary

Teachers

EMMA PACKARD, NICK PACKARD AND
SALLY BROWN

**KOGAN
PAGE**

London • Stirling (USA)

First published in 1997

Kogan Page Limited
120 Pentonville Road
London N1 9JN
and
22883 Quicksilver Drive
Stirling, VA 20166, USA

© Emma Packard, Nick Packard and Sally Brown, 1997

British Library Cataloguing in Publication Data

A CIP record for this book is available from the British Library.

ISBN 0 7494 2371 4

Typeset by Jo Brereton, Primary Focus, Haslington, Cheshire
Printed and bound in Great Britain by Clays Ltd, St Ives plc

500 Tips from Kogan Page

Dedication

We would like to dedicate this book to the many people who have helped us to learn and to develop over the years, but especially to John Pellowe who helped us to learn the most important lessons of all; despite his protestations, the truest of teachers.

EP and NP

Contents

Acknowledgements

We would like to thank the following for their comments and suggestions on this book: Mary Easterby, Ciaran Hannon, Geoff Mitchell, Evelyn Mitchell, Donna Gilberg, Jill Garrett, John Butler and Allison Thomson. Special thanks are due to Phil Race for his text management and patience.

Introduction

Don't read this book cover to cover in one sitting. That is not how it has been designed to be used. This is not a theoretical text covering complex issues or arcane intellectual matters. Instead it is a pragmatic dip-in text designed primarily to help newly qualified and student school teachers as well as those who feel in need of refreshment to get the most from their teaching.

These tips are based on the experiences of the authors, our colleagues and friends, over a number of years in the classroom, and we aim to offer a number of practical pointers, often hard won in the school of experience. We hope these will be helpful to you and will build on the work you have already undertaken as part of your training as a teacher.

Obviously, the range of children's abilities will vary enormously across the primary school and across the age range, so you will need to be selective about tips, choosing those that best fit your own particular context, leaving aside those ideas that don't seem appropriate for your own classes.

Use the book as a resource to check out ways of tackling problems you encounter, to provide alternative ideas on how to undertake a range of tasks, and to reassure yourself that lots of other people often encounter the same kinds of difficulties that you experience. We hope you will find it useful.

Contact us care of our publisher if you have any comments or suggestions for future imprints.

Emma Packard
Nick Packard
Sally Brown

Chapter 1   Classroom Management and Organisation

When working with young children the way that you set up and run a teaching space is crucial. Young children need to be clear about what is expected of them and how they are supposed to go about their work. A disorganised classroom or constantly changing routines make for chaotic lessons. This chapter contains some ideas on how to help ensure that your classroom and classroom organisation make life as easy and stress free as possible, for you *and* the children in your class. This section covers:

1   Preparing yourself for a lesson
2   Preparing the children for a lesson
3   Organising an integrated day
4   Providing for practical activities
5   Providing for consolidatory activities
6   Keeping children on task
7   Involving children
8   Different teaching styles
9   Using other adults in the classroom
10 Using other professionals in the classroom
11 Displaying work

1

Preparing yourself for a lesson

To ensure that you use the time you have with the children in school as efficiently as possible, you have to be sure that you are properly prepared. This chapter looks at a range of issues you may need to consider and gives some practical ideas for helping you to do this quickly and effectively.

1   **Always start positively.** In all aspects of your work, try to approach everything as cheerfully as possible. It usually has a positive effect on those around you too. Children are quick to pick up on a negative atmosphere and often react badly to it.

2   **Know where you are starting from.** This helps to ensure that activities and questions can be pitched at the right level. Once you have had a class for a short time you will quickly develop a good idea of your class's abilities and knowledge. Experience of a year group also counts for a lot, but in the meantime it may help to ask regular class teachers (if you are on teaching practice) or previous class teachers for background data. Also, refer to previous work and records of the children involved. Of course you could also start by asking the children!

3   **Know where you are going.** In your long-term planning you will have identified your long-term aims for a topic or term, but it is also essential to identify very short-term objectives for each activity or lesson. Know in advance exactly what you are hoping the children will have learned by the end of the lesson. This helps you to focus on the sorts of questions, resources and support you may need to build into the activity.

4   **Know what resources you will need.** Consider what resources will make the activity you are working on easier to manage and give appropriate structure so that the children can work independently, if necessary, helping to keep them on task.

5   **Know where to find these resources.** Much of what you will need for your lesson will be readily available in school. Ask subject coordinators where possible about specific resources. Sometimes your own ideas can be adapted to fit the resources available, but if not, you will need to either produce some resources yourself or delegate the task to auxiliaries or trainees, if you have them in school. (Ensure that you give *precise* instructions.)

6   **Allow plenty of time to set up.** Having all activities fully prepared and the resources readily available for the children before you begin the lesson will mean that they can settle to their work quickly. Even sharpening the pencils before the lesson means less fuss when the lesson starts. This is not always appropriate because children do need to learn how to organise themselves too, and this should be planned for.

7   **Make a list of the main points to be included in the lesson.** A list of the main points you wish to cover in discussions with the children, or instructions you need to give, can help you put your original intentions into practice, even though this is not always that easy.

8   **Decide who will work where.** Know where *you* will be working (your focus task). If you have nursery nurses, auxiliaries or parents helping in class, make sure you know what they are going to be doing too. You will need to give them clear and explicit instructions to make the best of their assistance.

9   **Have backup activities to hand.** Consider what those children who might finish their work early will do. Try to build extension activities into the normal routines of the day. Having role-play areas, structured work in sand and water or free writing areas, reading or number games, fiction and non-fiction books applicable to the class you are teaching readily available, will ensure that children are engaged in worthwhile activities while others finish off.

10 **Have a checklist that shows the activities individual children or groups of children will be working on**. It can also show when they start and whether they have finished or not. It will help you keep track and is especially useful if you are running an integrated day.

2

Preparing the children for a lesson

Getting the children in your class prepared for work is essential to get the best from them in the time available. The following ideas might help you to get the children settled and paying attention with the minimum of fuss.

1   **Welcome the children in to the class.** This gives you a chance to set the tone of the day. You will be able to welcome them properly but also to establish control and reinforce your expectations of them from the first moment.

2   **Settle the children down.** Many classrooms have a collecting or carpeted area, a place to gather the children together for whole class work and administration. Make clear to the class the rules that apply to the use of these areas. Having story or non-fiction books, puzzles, puppets or toys and some simple games available for the children in these areas gives them something to do and helps prevent disruptive behaviour.

3   **Manage things they might bring from home.** Matters that the children are likely to want to talk about, or items they may wish to play with, will cause disruption if they keep hold of things they have brought with them into class. If you want to encourage children to bring things into class for 'show and tell' sessions, have a space where they might leave their belongings or ask them to leave them in drawers.

4   **Establish the rules for registration.** Be imaginative: registration times can be fun and educational, but you will need to be clear and consistent about the rules. Try allowing children to respond in different languages or accents, quietly or loudly, time how long the register takes, or even sing responses, and so on.

5   **Set the scene for an activity**. Start with what the children already know. Sometimes an activity will build on previous work, so remind the children of this work. Introducing new ideas will require more discussion, so allow time for this and consider how best to introduce the idea. Often stories, books or artefacts can be used, but asking children what they already know about a concept also establishes a context well.

6   **Ensure the children know *why* they are doing what they are doing.** Making sure that children know what they are supposed to learn helps them to focus on the real point of the activity. Leaving them unsure of what they are trying to achieve means they might get the wrong end of the stick.

7   **Recap on the instructions you have given.** It is worth recapping on the main points of the activity the children will be tackling just before they start. With young children, try to keep the number of different instructions to a minimum.

8   **Give the children the chance to ask questions.** It's a good idea to let the children have the opportunity to check things out if they do not understand what is required of them. You can use this to reinforce the need for them to pay attention. Making it clear that you will not repeat your instructions once the lesson has started encourages good listening skills.

9   **Send the children to their jobs.** Getting the children to settle to their work quickly sets the right tone for the lesson. Sending them off in small groups, or even one by one, helps prevent a crush or arguments over who might sit where. It is worth spending the first few minutes ensuring the children make a good start on their work before getting on with your main focus activity.

10   **Consider the environmental needs of the children.** If the classroom is too warm or too cold, it makes it harder for them to concentrate. Try to get this sorted out before the lesson starts. Every so often, remind the children about others' needs and how important it is to let everyone get on with their work in peace.

3

Organising an integrated day

An integrated approach to classroom management is valuable because it can help children to balance independent learning with a more structured approach. Usually running an integrated day means tackling three or four activities, covering different areas of the curriculum at the same time. If you are going to use this integrated approach it is usually best to do it on a regular basis so that children get into the routines involved. The following tips offer some routines that might be useful.

1   **Have one focus activity for each work session.** One of the main advantages of integrated activities is that you can structure each work session so that you can work with a small group on a specific task – the thing that you are actually going to teach. Let the children know where you are going to be working too.

2   **Prepare other work for the rest of the class.** On the whole, these activities should be consolidatory tasks. Try to plan activities that the children will be able to tackle independently. Consider what resources you will be able to give the children to support them.

3   **Organise your classroom for integrated activities.** If you are going to work on integrated activities, your classroom will probably need to be set up in areas where resources that support work in each curriculum area can be collected and made available for the children. You might also want to try to separate potentially noisy or active areas from areas for quieter and more settled activities.

4   **Help the children to help you.** To allow you to get on with your focus activity, it is a good idea to instruct in advance those working on other tasks where they should put finished work and what they should do when they have finished, so as to avoid disturbing you. To help them manage their time it is also a good idea, now and then, to let them know how long they have got left.

5   **Remember that not every area of the curriculum has to be tackled each day or even each week**. Trying to squeeze everything into a space where it doesn't comfortably fit might result in a waste of time for all concerned. A half-term plan should allow a balance of learning across the curriculum.

6   **Be aware that administration of integrated days can be complex.** This is because you have to keep track of a range of different activities at the same time. Having a tick list that tables each child against each activity is virtually essential, as is a key that shows when they do what and how far they have progressed.

7   **Think about group sizes.** Generally it is easier to split up your class according to broad ability bands, but some activities are inappropriate for (say) ten children to do at once. Practical activities, scientific investigations, art work, technology and so on may need to be done in smaller groups, so consider what the others might be doing at the same time.

8   **Keep instructions simple.** Some children will need to work fairly independently. It is easy to bombard them with too much information. Often there will be points during work on your focus task where you can leave the children in your group to carry on independently. With careful management, you can use these times to give new briefings or reinforce previously delivered instructions or guidance to the other groups or mark work.

9   **Remember that setting up for integrated days can be time consuming.** This is because there are more activities to set up than when all of the children are working on one task. Try taking some of the pressure off and getting the children to set up the more practical tasks for you. If they have just done a particular activity they will have a fair idea of what is required and, besides, they love doing it.

10   **Make sure you finish the session as carefully as you started it.** At the end of the session you will probably want to get the children to start tidying up while you try to get round and check work. Having containers and spaces for storage of the equipment they have been using is really useful because it takes away a lot of the pressure of continually giving instructions about where things should go.

4

Providing for practical activities

The sorts of practical activity that you will want to tackle in your class obviously depend on the age of the children, the number in the class and how settled they tend to be, but there are still some basic, underlying ideas that might help you to organise and manage practical work. For ease they have been arranged into the three sections that practical activities tend to fall, but there is some overlap. It may also be useful to consider the ideas outlined in 'Organising an Integrated Day' too, (see page 8).

Scientific Investigation

1 **Provide unstructured opportunities for investigation**. Giving the children the materials that they will be investigating as a 'choosing' activity some time before setting a more structured one gives them a good head start when it comes to trying to answer a specific question. (For instance, leave out a range of batteries, wires and bulbs for a week or so, then ask them to try to make a circuit.)

2 **Try to make sure that there is an adult to help.** Left to their own devices, children tend to stray from an intended path during investigations. This may be part of the point, but if you or another adult can be on hand to ask questions and listen to the children's responses you will be able to keep the children focused on the original question.

3 **Consider whether you really need a written record from children.** Getting children to record an experiment (what the children observe and appear to find out) does not necessarily demonstrate understanding and can disrupt the children's concentration. A verbal report to the class, group

recording using an adult as a scribe, a concept keyboard overlay on a computer, diagrams, Cloze procedures, cut and stick activities, and so on, can be effective too.

4   **Manage investigations to keep children on task.** You may want a small number of them to experiment as a group and without adult support. Keeping them on task will need structuring. This could be achieved by the use of work sheets, prompt cards, peer tutoring or something even more imaginative, such as displays or games.

Mathematical Investigation

5   **Remember, you can never have too much practical equipment for maths.** This is especially true when working with very young children, and having this equipment on display and accessible to the children is also important. Small children may well find waiting their turn for equipment detrimental to attention and behaviour.

6   **Try to make practical activities relevant to children's lives.** If you want to tackle non-standard measures, comparing the height of the children, their hand spans, foot sizes, reach and so on, or comparing spoons, chairs, beds or even eating porridge from different bowls after reading *Goldilocks and the Three Bears* is more relevant and memorable than 'colouring the biggest bowl in the picture'.

Art and Technology

7   **Give the children ready access to materials that are available.** If they are able to get at what they need when they need it, they will not have to bother you so often. Set up your areas with as wide a range of materials on show as possible. In the long term this will also give them more confidence in choosing appropriate materials.

8   **For specific artistic activities, you will need to prepare the materials in advance.** If the table is ready for them to get on with their work they will settle more quickly and it will tend to be less messy and a more efficient use of time. When preparing these resources bear in mind the intended outcome.

9   **When working on developing specific skills, select specific resources.** If you want children to work on colour mixing or cutting out in a focused practical task, selecting materials for them in advance will help them achieve the intended outcomes and avoid waste.

10 **Allow access to plenty of materials when working on design-and-making activities.** Where the task is more open-ended and the children have the opportunity to experiment, investigate and solve problems, a wider range of materials should be available. It may be worth taking the time to discuss some of these materials with the children, including their properties, how to join and cut them, and how to avoid waste.

11 **Be creative about storage and display of resources.** Paint can be stored in screw-top coffee jars and used for less delicate activities where freshly mixed paint is not required.

12 **Be aware that storage styles affect how children use resources.** Where lots of materials are seen to be available, children tend to use them faster. Materials that are displayed in interesting ways inspire children.

5

Providing for consolidatory activities

Well thought-out and structured consolidatory tasks are essential if they are going to be beneficial to the children and allow you the time to concentrate on your focus task. The following are some tried and tested ideas for effective consolidatory activities.

1   **Remember the importance of work sheets.** Just because it's on an A4 piece of paper, does not mean it is 'death by worksheet'. Well-planned and interesting worksheets help to structure work for young children. They can keep children on task, help them to concentrate and work with relatively little support and so assist you to achieve your aims.

2   **Be aware of the alternatives to work sheets.** Work cards might be more appropriate. If the activity requires something to keep the children focused on their work but doesn't have to help them structure the way they record their answers, a work card, backed in clear plastic, or laminated to protect it, can be very effective and efficient because it can be used over and over again, year after year.

3   **Collect together open-ended resources.** A set of cards with the letters of the alphabet, numbers 0 to 20, common initial letter blends or digraphs, sight vocabulary words, days, times, seasons and so on are useful time and again and can be used for a wide range of consolidatory activities without the need for new resources.

4   **Try to get a stock of open-ended work sheets.** Work sheets with no single specific purpose, like blank 100 squares or number pyramids, domino squares, alphabet ladders and so on are invaluable in a range of contexts. Having a stock of as many of these sorts of work sheets as possible and a wide repertoire of activities to go with them means you will never be without something useful to give to the children.

5 **Collect jigsaws, dominoes, playing cards, dice and other such activity resources.** They are useful, worthwhile and familiar activities you will use time and time again, in a variety of educational ways.

6 **Children can design and make their own games.** If you have been studying a particular concept in number work or phonics, for example, asking the children to design and make a game about that idea is not only a worthwhile activity, but also a demonstration of exactly what the children have understood about the work you have been doing. It may even produce more resources for the rest of the class.

7 **Recycle resources used in structured activities.** If you have produced resources for an activity to introduce a new concept, you might be able to recycle them for use on a work sheet (for example, pictures on initial letter dominoes could be copied and used on work cards or sheets).

8 **Experiment with peer tutoring.** There can be benefits for both parties. Often, when particular children have grasped a concept, then a good way of consolidating their ideas is by getting them to try to explain it to others who are still struggling. Sometimes they do it even better than a teacher, because they have the relevant perspective on the concept which helps the struggler too.

9 **Share ideas with colleagues.** If you work in a school with more than one class to each year group try sharing ideas and resources with the parallel class teacher. You could even split up the jobs to cover twice the ground.

10 **Use homework to consolidate skills or concepts covered in class.** This opens up opportunities for parents or carers to tune in to the ways you are working with the children. It is best not to introduce new concepts in homework activities, as you may find that the approach adopted by parents in not in line with your planned way of covering them. As far as possible, involve parents and carers in understanding the purposes of homework and what you are trying to achieve.

6

Keeping children on task

If you can keep children on task during work sessions, then you can avoid disruption and get on with what you really need to do. But juggling 30-odd children and three or four different activities is no mean feat. The following suggestions offer some ideas to help with this.

1   **Try to keep to routines.** Children usually like and respond well to routine. If children know what to expect, they tend to stay more settled and concentrate better. As far as possible, try to develop routines for the everyday activities and stick to them.

2   **Develop rules to encourage good work habits.** Making rules clear, concise and explicit so the children know what is expected of them is an important part of developing their 'social responsibility'. Sometimes children just fail to notice that their behaviour has a significant effect on the rest of the class.

3   **Try to group the children to avoid confrontation.** Some children just cannot work together. It isn't always easy, but try to group children so that they are sitting and working with children with whom they get on well, but avoid them becoming over-excited.

4   **Make the work appropriate and relevant.** This can make a great deal of difference to classroom management. If children are working on tasks that they can manage, but that they find interesting, then they will settle quickly and concentrate for longer. It is worth taking time to plan and differentiate your activities carefully because, in the long run, it will make your life a lot easier.

5   **Develop good time-keeping skills.** If children are clear about how long they have to finish a task, and you reinforce this throughout work times by letting them know how much time is remaining, it will help them to work more consistently. It's worth letting them know what the consequences of not finishing might be!

6 **Explain why they are doing what they are doing.** If children know what they are supposed to be learning or finding out about, it makes them more confident and so keeps them interested and motivated. Before they go about their work, tell them what you expect them to achieve.

7 **Consider your responses.** The responses you give to the children about their work are obviously really important and provide a good opportunity for motivating the class. A tick and a 'well done' is fine for everyday but there are many much more imaginative responses. These include star badges, certificates, special jobs, showing work to the rest of the class, showing work to other teachers or to the headteacher, as well as your own comments in response to achievements. The list of tried and tested ways of keeping children interested is endless. (See also section 'Marking work and giving feedback', Chapter 5.)

8 **Keep tasks short and sweet.** Some children have real problems con-centrating for sustained periods. They may need specific help, and talking to your school's special educational needs coordinator is usually helpful. In the meantime, keeping tasks short, specific, familiar, but as stimulating and achievable as possible will help them to stay on task, and children's ensuing successes may help improve their self-esteem.

9 **Try to be aware of the whole class.** Even if you are working on one specific activity, going round and checking work, praising effort and tackling minor problems will reassure children and remind them that what they are doing is still important.

10 **Offer praise and encouragement.** No teacher should be above a bit of 'bribery and corruption'! Setting goals and offering rewards, however simple, can have a positive effect on children's motivation to work.

7

Involving children

Ideas of ownership are closely linked to effective teaching and learning. The whole process is essentially about empowering children and helping them to play a role in their own learning. The following suggestions will possibly include many of the things that you already do in the classroom, but perhaps will give you additional ideas to build on.

1   **Work out as many different ways as possible for children to make inputs into your teaching and their learning.** For example, you could have daily or weekly targets. It will be up to the children to decide when and how they work towards them, but insist that they must do them.

2   **Show children that you value their views.** When children make suggestions that are not sensible, don't reject them out of hand, but acknowledge them and then get the children to suggest how their ideas might be adapted to fit the circumstances better. Build on what they say rather than destroy their confidence.

3   **Get children to brainstorm ideas in class.** Even when starting a new topic, it is useful to involve the class in a brainstorm to collect together the existing knowledge and ideas about the subject. This will give you a clearer idea of where they are starting from, and developing their sense of ownership will help them to focus on the work in hand.

4   **Collect feedback from children.** Find out from them details of what they enjoy, and why they enjoy it. Similarly, find out what they dislike and why they dislike it. Then use this to inform the decisions that you make about classroom activities.

5   **Try to respond positively to any suggestions children make.** Explain to them what you have done in response to their suggestions, or why it has not be possible to do so. Involving them in this way is likely to have a positive effect on their motivation.

6   **Let children set their own deadlines for pieces of work.** It might be possible to let children negotiate with you how long a piece of work may take – if you know them well! Considering what will be required and how much time they will need is an excellent way to help them learn about forward planning and will encourage them to work to deadlines. It may also act as a great motivator. Be prepared to let them renegotiate, however, if they have been over- (or under-) ambitious in their targets.

7   **Let children get involved in assessing each others' work.** Children will learn a great deal from seeing and discussing their peers' work, good or bad. Obviously it is important to prepare the ground for such an activity. For instance, you might agree with the children on how to phrase criticism positively, on avoiding using personal remarks, and on backing up criticism with evidence to avoid hurting anyone's feelings.

8   **Involve children in helping each other to learn.** The process of working with other children is as beneficial for those leading as for those following. Not only will less able pupils learn from the guidance of others, but also the more able are likely to benefit from the reinforcement they derive from explaining things to someone else.

9   **Children can help to evaluate learning resource materials.** Children are likely to be able to tell you the strengths and weaknesses of learning materials and computer packages. The feedback they provide is based on usage by the target group that the materials were designed for, so is likely to be very sound.

10 **Get children involved in daily administrative tasks.** It is useful to let children take responsibility for daily routines such as preparing the milk, returning the register, tidying up, watering plants, and sharpening pencils. This can help them to develop good working habits and build up their sense of responsibility, as well as making them feel good about themselves. You can organise rotas so no one gets left out. Never underestimate the seriousness with which children will approach their tasks.

8

Different teaching styles

How effectively you teach is closely related to how you choose to teach, and the ways in which you feel most comfortable working. Whole class teaching currently has a high profile, but different teaching styles are clearly going to be more appropriate for teaching certain concepts than others. Most of the time you will know almost instinctively what is and is not an appropriate way of tackling something, but here are a few ideas about how certain teaching styles can be used effectively.

1   **Make the most of whole class opportunities.** Use them to develop whole class cohesion as well as for giving instruction, giving demonstrations and asking general questions. Children like to feel part of a group, and the times when you are working with the class as a whole are the ones where they will develop collective cohesiveness.

2   **Children can learn by doing in large groups.** Even as a whole class, children can be given tasks to do independently for a few minutes at a time. This will help to break up the session and maintain attentiveness.

3   **Whole class sessions can be used to help children to make sense of the things they have already learned**. Through the process of discussing a task and what people found out, think or have learned, children's confidence will grow as they see that their ideas fit in with those of others. Of course, they could also realise that they have got the wrong end of the stick and usefully ask for help.

4   **Feedback can be drawn from children in whole class sessions.** Such sessions can be used to provide a useful barometer of how their learning is progressing. Well-directed and carefully phrased questions will give you an opportunity to make some useful assessments, both for individuals and groups.

5　**Put energy and effort into making your whole class sessions interesting and stimulating.** A well-paced and structured session, that has some visual impact and which involves the children, is a powerful teaching opportunity. It is the kind of occasion that children remember for years to come, and can be really stimulating for teachers too.

6　**Think about the different ways of forming groups.** These include randomly, alphabetically, by friendship, by ability or mixed ability. Each method has its advantages and its drawbacks. Try to use a system that suits you and that suits the children. Don't change the groups round so often that the children are unsettled, but provide opportunities for them to work in different groupings, so that they get used to the idea.

7　**Help children in their early attempts at collaborative work.** Children don't always naturally work well in groups. Try to manage such work so that you have the chance to help them to assist and cooperate with one another, rather than fight over who does what and when. With a little guidance they can often achieve very productive outcomes.

8　**Try to ensure a balance of participation.** It is important that everyone has the opportunity to gain from and participate in group work. You will always have both dominant and retiring children in any group, but with careful management, you should be able to give everyone a chance. Try directing questions at individuals and start with the more confident ones who appear to know what is going on. This gives the less confident children a chance to watch and learn from the others. Start directing questions at those children when they start showing more interest.

9　**Try to manufacture opportunities for one-to-one work.** Working with individual children is important in all kinds of situations, particularly, for example, when hearing them read, and when they are having particular difficulties. If you can get children working independently on familiar tasks, take whatever chances you can to work in this way. You may consider giving up some break times to work with individuals, and may be able to negotiate that you are excused from some assemblies.

10　**Have rules that allow you to work uninterrupted.** Opportunities to work one-to-one during class time have to be planned for and become part of normal classroom routines. Get children used to the idea that you have work to do too, and they should only approach you under certain, predetermined circumstances.

9

Using other adults in the classroom

No matter how good you are, you can always use another pair of hands. Some schools have additional auxiliary support, but encouraging governors, parents, grandparents and others to help out too can really reap dividends. (See also 'Working with outside agencies' in Chapter 6.) It can also be tricky, but thorough preparation will pay off in terms of additional support for you in your teaching, which can be absolutely invaluable.

1   **You may need to give volunteers quite detailed information.** This is likely to be about the level and kinds of support you want the children to have, or the intended outcomes of the activity. You may need to give guidance about the sorts of questions they should ask or how they might help children to reach a greater understanding of the work they are doing. Making sure they know what they are doing, and why, will mean that you get the best help possible.

2   **Find out what you can about the people who offer to help.** Try to get to know the parents or carers of the children in your class before asking for help, or try asking the class's previous teacher for suggestions. With the best will in the world, not every parent will make the ideal helper in class and asking ones with whom you think you are likely to work well may make life a bit easier.

3   **Check your school's policy on having volunteers in class.** Often volunteers need police clearance before being allowed to work with children, and it is essential you check this out. It's worth going through all the proper procedures, to ensure that your children are in safe hands.

4 **Check your school's policy on having volunteers *out* of the class.** Asking volunteers to take groups or individuals out of the class or to work in the school grounds or in the local community is usually only acceptable if they are helping you to supervise a group, but again, check your school's policy first. It is best to err on the side of caution.

5 **Build a good working relationship with volunteers.** It is a good idea to ask them what sorts of activities they might like to work on. If they are enjoying it, the children they work with are more likely to enjoy it too. You can also build on the strengths they can offer, to get the best from the process.

6 **Get adult helpers to come in a little before the session starts**. This will give you time to introduce them to the activity they will be helping with, and you will be able to consider and discuss the activity properly without interruptions. It will also provide time for them to ask questions and to voice their opinions.

7 **If you feel a volunteer is not coping with some activities, try something else**. They might struggle working with a group of ten children on a structured task, but have a whale of a time in one-to-one activities developing phonemic awareness or 'number bonds'. It's difficult to tackle a subject like this from cold, so experimenting with activities until you find something that suits you both can be a diplomatic solution.

8 **Remember that no helper needs to be redundant.** Getting them involved in mounting work, preparing resources, stocking shelves or baskets of resources are always good uses of volunteers' time. Try to save up jobs you can delegate for the times when you have help in the classroom.

9 **At the end of the session, make sure that the children and the volunteers know who is doing what.** Out of a willingness to be as helpful as possible, volunteers may end up doing jobs that you would prefer the children to do. Clarifying the tasks at the outset will avoid confusion.

10 **Remember, you are in charge.** The discipline in the class is still your responsibility and if some children working with a volunteer are not behaving as you would expect them to, it's a good idea to just bite the bullet and treat that group in the same way as you would normally, otherwise they may start to take advantage of the situation. More often than not, volunteers and parents appreciate the fact that you supporting them in their voluntary efforts.

11   **Be careful about what you ask helpers in the classroom to do.** You need to estimate carefully how best to balance the help offered to you. Some parents/carers may take exception if they feel unqualified helpers are 'teaching' their children.

12   **Consider how you can best use governors in the classroom.** For example, in some schools each class 'adopts' a particular governor who then tries to get involved with the class as much as possible. This can also provide an excellent channel of communication between the school and the governors.

10

Using other professionals in the classroom

Getting the best out of an experienced nursery nurse, auxiliary or student involves developing a different working relationship from those required for working well with parents and volunteers. These tips relate largely to working with a nursery nurse on a full- or half-time basis, but can also be extended to other professionals working with you in the classroom.

1   **Plan your programme of study together**. This is important when working with fellow professionals, even if they are less qualified than yourself. For them to work effectively, they have to know what you are both trying to achieve and, ideally, to agree with those goals too.

2   **Share responsibility for the everyday chores.** A nursery nurse, for example, is not there just to do the messy jobs that you don't like doing. If you share out the unpleasant jobs you can share out the nice ones too. This way you will develop a genuine, productive working partnership.

3   **Use your respective strengths and interests.** By playing to your strengths, the two of you will be able to cover far more of the curriculum much more effectively. Enthusiasm is infectious and the children will get more out of an activity when the person teaching them is enjoying it too.

4   **Share ideas about the design and maintenance of children's records.** Assistants who know what is needed and why it is needed in children's records, will be better placed to assist you in the collection and filing of evidence. It is important that everyone works to the same system, or confusion can arise.

5   **Visit other schools together.** You may be able to pick up new ideas or discuss solutions to problems that you are experiencing, and it may be a pleasant team-building outing for both of you.

6   **Build in opportunities to review your work together.** Feedback from other trained professionals about how things are going, and where they could go to next, is invaluable. You will find that you can achieve more than twice as much as you would have done on your own.

7   **Approach your headteacher about possible training opportunities.** These opportunities should relate to the development of the team. It is important that co-professionals have the chance to get involved in the development of your unit.

8   **Use your nursery nurse's previous experience.** They may well have tackled issues or aspects of the curriculum that you haven't, and nothing counts so much as having been through it before. Make the most of your colleague's ideas, and value contributions from each other.

9   **Make sure you both have the chance of doing something different.** Variety is the spice of life and a break from an activity or responsibility can do you both good. Taking turns with activities can stop them becoming monotonous, and it also means that you can cover for each other in emergencies.

10   **Use whole group times effectively.** How many teachers are needed when the children are watching television or hearing a story? It could be that these times will provide good opportunities for getting other things done, with only one person supervising the whole group.

11   **Consider team teaching.** Where you have the resources to manage this, team teaching can be an enormously creative and enjoyable method of sharing work in the classroom.

11

Displaying work

Displaying work is important as it can be used as a focus for discussion, a stimulus for creative work, a recognition of children's achievements and an opportunity to enhance the classroom environment. It may be the most valuable resource you can have.

1   **Have a variety of ways and spaces for displaying work.** Don't just consider what you are going to put on which wall but how tables, benches, boxes, shelves, fabrics and so on can be used to make the best of a space.

2   **Mount work before displaying it.** Work looks significantly better when it is mounted, though whether it is single or double mounted may be determined by availability of resources. You could consider mounting on different sorts of materials: cardboard, tin foil, Christmas wrapping paper, unused wallpaper, fabrics and so on. You can also consider whether you really want everything to be rectangular or not.

3   **Plan displays for 3D work carefully**. Think of creative or unusual ways of displaying work. For example you might try making stacks of cardboard boxes and draping them with fabric (secured with twists of masking tape). Or you could attach small boxes to walls (though staples tend to be problematic) to make small shelves, or hang models from strings stapled to the walls or attached to the ceiling, or make use of benches, window ledges, and shelves. Whatever you do is likely to have to suffer small pedestrianised traffic, so try to build it to last.

4   **Use display work for language development.** Displays can be used as a good way of consolidating or even extending children's understanding of activities they have been working on. Captions to accompany displayed work can explain processes, ask questions, add descriptive detail and generate added interest. They can offer support to reading, written and number work and discussion in ways that can be very productive.

5   **Use interactive displays as a stimulus**. Displays can be used as a stimulus and a support for investigative or creative work. For instance, as a class, make a map on the wall of the route of Rosie's Walk in the story of the same name, and then use it to help the children to sequence the events in the story. Involving as many children as possible can help them to feel part of the process.

6   **Use different kinds of text.** Different sizes and styles of lettering, and different kinds of written information, such as newspaper articles, typed or handwritten captions by you or the children, letters cut out of different coloured papers or fabrics, all help to enhance the impact of a display as well as to extend awareness of the written word.

7   **Use your displays.** Encourage children to notice, describe and comment upon them. For instance, 'What have we put on the wall? Why has it been displayed there? How has it been displayed and what do you think of it? How would you have done it? What do you like and what would you like to change?'

8   **Site permanent classroom displays where they will do the most good.** If you have a number line in the class, try to put it where the children working in number can see it. Have book displays in a corner where children can sit quietly; you could also have a couple of comfortable chairs and a listening centre there.

9   **Make collections of artefacts.** They are an excellent stimulus but, whether collected by you or the children, they need to be sited in a safe place and children will need to be given specific instructions on what they are allowed to touch and how to handle objects safely. Restricting their interest by stopping them from touching may seem a shame, but it is also important that they know how to treat other people's belongings. Don't forget the safety implications of displays.

10 **Try to establish displays that evolve over time.** These sorts of displays tend to hold children's attention for longer and should be referred to and discussed on a regular, even daily, basis. Children will enjoy watching a display as it changes and develops, and will learn from the experience too.

Chapter 2   Curricular Responsibilities

Very few primary teachers are just concerned with what is going on in their own classrooms and, if they were, that would surely be to their detriment. Most teachers will be given additional responsibility for specific areas of the curriculum or school life, which obviously raises a number of issues, not least how to find the time. Different schools will have very different expectations of curriculum coordinators, as will individual members of staff, so you will need to find ways to balance the needs of the school, the needs of your colleagues, the needs of the children and most importantly, your own needs. This section covers:

12   Managing time
13   Coordinating a curriculum area
14   Covering the National Curriculum
15   Ensuring progression and continuity
16   Extra-curricular activities
17   Getting the most from In-Service Training (INSET)
18   Offering In-Service Training (INSET)
19   Communicating with colleagues
20   Policies and schemes of work
21   Making learning processes meaningful to children
22   Planning a new topic

12

Managing time

No matter how efficient you are, any teacher could end up working 24 hours a day, seven days a week. This chapter suggests some ideas to help you make the best use of your time so that you can do what you need to do for your class and still have enough time for yourself at the end of the day. It may help preserve your sanity too!

1   **Leave time for yourself.** It is easy to get into the habit of working all the hours available, but enough is enough. If all you do is work, then you may well limit the enthusiasm and experiences you can bring into the classroom. Don't feel guilty about having some evenings and parts of weekends to yourself.

2   **Get yourself an action plan.** If you can set yourself a detailed but realistic plan of the things you would like to cover in a topic, term, or year, as a subject coordinator or whatever, and then stick to it, it will help you use your time effectively.

3   **Be aware that action plans go wrong.** This is probably because you cannot predict what might happen. If it becomes obvious that you are not going to be able to live up to your aspirations, for whatever reason, it's better to adapt or make a new plan than to work yourself silly to keep up. The best action plans are strict enough to keep you to task, but flexible enough to cope with contingencies.

4   **Set aside time in school for coordinating your area of the curriculum.** Try to decide upon a time during your week, probably after school, when you can support or meet with colleagues, check and order resources, and do similar tasks. Training yourself and your colleagues to use this time effectively helps.

5   **Organise your subject resources**. Doing this so that you know what materials and resources you have got, and where they are, will help you to respond to the needs of your curriculum area efficiently. Persuading colleagues to maintain this organisation helps even more.

6   **Try to be proactive rather than reactive in the ways you communicate with others.** This is perhaps most important when responding to enquiries or relevant issues. Informing the whole staff at once rather than one by one is more efficient, and keeping them up to date with what you are doing may help to solve issues before they arise. If you know where you are going, it makes responding to issues or questions easier.

7   **Delegate whatever you reasonably can.** They say that delegation is the key to good management. Before doing something yourself, consider whether you can give the job to nursery nurses, auxiliaries, administrative assistants, trainees, parents and even children. This may help by taking some of the pressure off you, and freeing up time for you to develop new activities and initiatives.

8   **Take time to check what resources and materials are already available in school.** It might save you having to make your own. While checking through resource cupboards and files will give you the information you need, try asking your colleagues first; it is quicker than wading through it all by yourself.

9   **Don't reinvent the wheel.** Even if the resources you can get hold of do not give you exactly what you want, they may be adaptable and could save you a lot of planning time, which is often the hardest bit. Be wary of the 'not invented here' syndrome, and be open to modifying resources when they are nearly what you want.

10   **Get the children active.** Children love the responsibility of sharpening pencils, bringing in the milk, emptying the water tray, taking messages, even photocopying work sheets, so let them. You might even be able to set up a helper-system in school, where the older children act as aids to teachers of younger children in lunch times, where this can be beneficial to all parties.

11   **Establish access to your headteacher informally as well as by invitation.** Don't feel as if you have to wait until asked, or until disaster strikes, before you approach your headteacher for advice and support. Investing a little of your time in maintaining good communication with your manager can save time and energy later on.

12   **Work out time-efficient ways of communicating with others.** Use staffroom encounters to keep people informed, and use Post-it notes and amendments to respond quickly to documents rather than feeling you have to provide a full written response.

13

Coordinating a curriculum area

Many primary or infant teachers are given an area of the curriculum, or an aspect of a school's management to coordinate. Sometimes this may be related to a personal interest or to an individual's educational background, but sometimes it isn't. In smaller schools, teachers may have responsibility for several aspects of school life. Whatever the set-up in your school, you will need to see that whatever you are coordinating is undertaken efficiently and professionally.

1   **Start with the resources.** It is a relatively manageable thing to tackle. Find out what you have got and where it is. Make a list or a catalogue. These can be useful for informing other staff about what is available and where it is. It will also help you to identify what you lack, so you can take steps to obtain what you need.

2   **Organise your resources.** If you have a designated storage area for your resources, sort them out and if possible get the school secretary to make up labels so that every box, shelf, drawer or cupboard says on the outside what it holds on the inside. This can save enormous amounts of time, especially if you can persuade the rest of the staff to put things back where they came from!

3   **Maintain resources for your curriculum area.** This is likely to be your responsibility. Some schools delegate parts of their budget to curriculum areas and others ask you to submit requisitions but, either way, a good place to start is by looking at last year's orders and, of course, at what you have got left.

4   **Consider how resources might help move your curriculum area forward.** Ask your colleagues what they think would help them to teach your subject. Looking through educational catalogues can also give you a few good ideas for opportunities for new activities. Be cautious, however, about buying resources without having a clear idea about using them.

5   **Get yourself trained**. It may come down to you to help support colleagues with the development of your curriculum area. Your local education authority and local universities will probably run educational training courses. Ask your headteacher about allowing you to attend some of these. They may not be exactly what you need, but just having the time to discuss ideas with others in the same situation can be very useful.

6   **Offer In-Service Training.** Running informal workshops can be a productive way of offering colleagues support. You may be called upon to offer your colleagues advice and training and, if you are keen to make improvements in your curricular area, you will have to put in a lot of effort. There is never enough time for training, but giving staff a chance to come to you by offering workshop sessions after school can help. Nowadays, some schools open these up to parents and governors too.

7   **Map out a progression of skills for your subject.** This can give you a good overview of what you are trying to achieve. With the help of management or experienced staff, sit down and plan the broad aspects of what children should experience in your subject across the whole school. This will help you to decide on realistic and achievable goals.

8   **Help staff to plan your subject carefully.** By developing activities that match the themes you have outlined in the progression charts, you can make sure that all the areas that you want to cover get covered. Detailed plans do not have to be inflexible, but should set out guidelines for action.

9   **Tackle one issue at a time.** Otherwise you end up juggling half a dozen different things at the same time and not really doing any of them properly. Finishing what you start can be tricky when there are so many other things to keep track of in a classroom. Keep aspects of your curricular responsibilities to small, manageable chunks.

10   **Tread carefully!** Other members of staff may not be as enthusiastic about changes and advice as you are yourself, not least because it may mean extra work. Diplomacy is essential if you want to achieve your goals. Take time to explain why you are trying to implement changes, and spell out to everyone details of the benefits that should accrue.

14

Covering the National Curriculum

Part of your responsibility as a class teacher is to ensure that the National Curriculum is delivered to the children in your class. The fact that your own education may not have equipped you to feel confident in teaching all the subjects in the National Curriculum can compound an already complex problem. So where do you find the support and information you need in order to do your job properly?

1   **Track down established schemes of work.** Some schools have a system of support that could map out what you teach and when you teach it. Though this may seem rather rigid, it does help a school to ensure that it offers exactly what it should. If your school works to this kind of system, get hold of schemes of work before you start planning.

2   **Establish the focus of a topic before you plan.** Different topics give opportunities for focusing on different subject areas. Before you plan, make sure you know what the intended focus of your topic is. The danger is that your provision will be diffused if you do not have a clear vision to start with.

3   **Find out if your school has already mapped out the curriculum areas.** If it has, then planning for activities that cover the skills and concepts that have already been mapped out for you will ensure that you are tackling activities that are worthwhile and that fit into an overall plan for each subject.

4   **If you do not have schemes of work, try to get hold of old planning and record sheets.** Ensuring that you are not needlessly repeating work that has already been covered in a previous class will be your responsibility. Check through these records to get an idea of what your class has already covered.

5   **Remember that a lot of the National Curriculum is just common sense.** Looking at the core subjects, if you have an idea about what the next step should be in helping the children to acquire the knowledge and skills they need to become competent at using numbers or language, then it will almost certainly fit with the National Curriculum.

6   **Find out what others are doing.** Comparing notes with other teachers, on how they are addressing areas of the National Curriculum, can be most helpful. You may then be in a position to return the favour with something that may be taxing your colleagues' ingenuity.

7   **Network wherever you can.** Talk about National Curriculum issues with colleagues you meet at training events, members of your social circle who are involved in primary school teaching, and others whose brains you can pick, to help you to make sense of the requirements.

8   **Get along to the library.** Read what others have written about implementing the National Curriculum. You may find journal articles, books and items on the Internet that will further familiarise you with what you need to know.

9   **Use the National Curriculum framework creatively.** Don't let it be a straitjacket, preventing you from introducing innovative ideas and approaches into your teaching. Explore ways in which you can satisfy the requirements in ways that fit your own context and individual approaches.

10 **You don't have to know the National Curriculum inside out to be able to teach it effectively.** Planning stimulating and appropriate experiences for the children will probably be more than adequate, and making these sorts of experience part of the normal daily or weekly routines will help you cover most of what you need to.

15

Ensuring continuity and progression

This is really a whole school issue, but nevertheless some schools don't tackle this effectively. You may still need to take steps to ensure that you are not repeating work your class has already done, and also ensure that what you plan will extend the children's skills and understanding, enabling them to make real progress.

1   **Make sure that you are familiar with the records that already exist.** You will need to build on prior achievement if you are to demonstrate children's progression from the baseline data.

2   **Get an idea of the range of abilities in the class.** A class's previous teacher may be able to give you an idea of the levels achieved by the more able, the average and the less able children in a class, and the sorts of work that the children could be expected to do next.

3   **Find out about the sorts of routine the children are used to.** Children, especially those who are less able, rely on and respond well to established routines. Work that is presented and tackled in a similar way but which extends children's knowledge is easier to manage in the classroom. Beware of boredom setting in though, and build in the unexpected from time to time.

4   **Establish the kinds of support materials they are used to.** Maintaining a consistent approach to supporting children's independent work makes things easier for you and less stressful for the children. If children are used to using number lines to 20 there is little point in giving them 100 squares and expecting them to be able to use them without introduction and support from you.

5   **Consider where they should be by the end of the year**. While knowing where the children are coming from is very important, discussing with a teacher in the year above where they should be by the end of the year might give you a better idea of what you are trying to achieve.

6   **Keep reasonably detailed records of what you have done.** These will be useful to hand on to your class's next teacher, who can then build on what you have started. Keeping such records can also help you to remember from year to year details of what you did, and may save you preparation time.

7   **Consider whether to group or not to group.** Grouping your class by ability is not universally regarded as ideal, but doing so may make it easier to differentiate the work you give children, and to provide the sorts of resources that support the way they need to work.

8   **Keep a tick list to help you to keep track.** A matrix listing of the children in your class, against the work that they have tackled, will help you to keep track of what they are doing and when, and will provide a really good record of what they have achieved for future reference.

9   **Concentrate on the basic skills.** This is especially important early on in the primary age range, where number and literacy skills can be developed in a fairly progressive way. Keeping track of what is going on here and where the work should go next is fairly simple. Concepts related to humanities or science can usefully stand much more repetition because they are not so developmental.

10 **Make sure that any repetition is deliberate.** Repeating activities and areas of work can provide useful consolidation, but repetition brought about because the teacher has no records of previous work is rarely beneficial.

16

Extra-curricular activities

Many schools offer a range of extra-curricular activities. Some offer them within the normal school timetable through club or activity sessions, and others offer opportunities outside the normal school day or at lunch times. Whichever your school offers may affect the amount of choice you have in whether or not to offer extra-curricular activities, and what kind you are likely to be involved in. In many schools there is a single person who coordinates extra-curricular activities, and you may want to discuss your role with that person. These tips are designed to help you make the most of the opportunity by asking the right kinds of question.

1 **Consider what you are going to do.** Just because you are good at something doesn't mean you necessarily want to spend your free time doing it with thirty lively, demanding children, so be selective about what you offer.

2 **Consider when you are going to do it.** Your time as a teacher is precious so don't offer too much at first. For example, football matches, leagues, cup ties, training and the like can take up vast amounts of time, so do not make too many commitments until you know you can keep them.

3 **Consider where you are going to do it.** Check with cleaners, caretakers and headteachers about whether your plans are going to interfere with theirs. Plans can be readily sabotaged by uncooperative support staff, so make sure that you take their needs into account from the outset.

4 **Consider how many are going to do it with you.** Pick a manageable number of children, and stick to it (always err on the side of caution). It's easy to get pressured into taking on more than you want to, and you need to ask yourself whether you and they will still enjoy it if you take on too many.

5   **Consider whether you have the space.** If you are running a creative activity, technology or art work, consider how much space you have available before deciding on the numbers that you intend to take on. Consider also where work might be stored from one week to the next. Sometimes your solutions to the space problem can be quite creative, however.

6   **Consider who might want to do it too.** Working alongside another member of staff is more fun and probably safer for you. Ask other members of staff if they would like to help out, and look for other potential helpers from your classroom volunteers.

7   **Consider who needs to know.** Obviously, the head, other teachers whose pupils might be involved and the parents or carers of those children will need to be aware of your plans. Most schools also insist that parents are informed of the arrangements in writing, and that you get permission slips from them.

8   **Consider whether you have a mission.** Setting yourself a goal, such as a performance or display, may seem like a good way of focusing your activities, but it can also become a pressure. Sometimes, just doing things for the fun of it is more enjoyable for both the children and for yourself, and less stressful for all concerned.

9   **Consider what you need to know.** You should check if your school has a policy on extra-curricular activities. If it has, read it, and try to ensure that your plan articulates with it. Ask yourself whether you will need any extra training, qualifications or additional insurance to lead the activities. Make sure you have made adequate provision for First Aid requirements.

10 **Think of the transport implications.** If you are running the activities after school, find out and record how the children will get home. Alternatively, if they are going to be picked up at school, find out who you can expect to collect them. It is also important to make sure you know they have indeed been picked up at the end of the evening.

17

Getting the most from In-Service Training (INSET)

Whether you are intending to benefit from In-Service Training from someone else, or hoping others will benefit from what you have to offer, INSET can be rather a hit or miss affair. But here are some things that you can do to avoid wasting time, yours or everybody else's.

1   **Identify your own developmental needs**. Despite pressures to the contrary, you can't be the perfect teacher in every aspect of the curriculum, so prioritise your own professional needs as far as you can. Do not be tempted to take training just because it is on offer. Make sure you think it is going to be worthwhile and relevant before you enrol.

2   **Seek help if you are not sure what your needs are.** Consult with your mentor or appointed appraiser, line manager or your close colleagues. You could also talk to your head or deputy or even your local education authority advisory teacher. They may be able to observe your teaching and make suggestions that help you identify your own needs. You will also get feedback sooner or later from your Office for Standards in Education (OFSTED) inspection.

3   **Ask your headteacher where the best place to get help might be.** It may be the case that support can be offered from within the school, from another member of staff who has received training or has experience in that particular field. Otherwise your local education authority advisory service or local further education colleges and universities may offer continuing professional development courses that are suitable.

4   **When reading details of courses, read the small print.** Read prospectuses from providers of training to make sure you know what the course will offer. Titles can be misleading, and you may well be limited to a fairly restricted number of courses per year for financial reasons. Make sure that the ones you choose are right for you.

5   **If the small print does not tell you enough, try to find out more.** Get in touch with the institution, or preferably the individual who will be running the course, to get clarification of exactly what is on offer and whether it will help you. This kind of research pays dividends in the long run.

6   **Ask other colleagues.** They may have attended similar courses on previous occasions or may have encountered the trainer before (especially where local education authority advisory service training is concerned) to find out if it's going to be worthwhile for you.

7   **Try to match your needs with what is on offer.** This will help to ensure you don't waste your own time and the school's resources on inappropriate training that does not cover your developmental needs. Consult with whoever is coordinating staff development in your school. This is likely to be your headteacher or a member of the senior management team. Remember that your needs for development will have to be tied in with the needs identified within the school development plan.

8   **Remember that if it's worth doing it's worth investing time in.** Attending a one-off course may help tackle immediate, short-term issues and raise your awareness, but it will not help raise your own skills all that much. Sometimes, only a concerted effort will suffice. Attending a series of courses after school, or reading relevant books, or giving yourself time to practise on a weekly basis will have a significant long-term impact.

9   **Use educational journals and magazines constructively.** They are often packed full with practical activities on how to develop specific ideas or skills in the classroom and, although they may not appear to be training materials in themselves, they often give you access to what the 'experts' consider good practice as well as tried and tested learning experiences for the children.

10 **Make use of informal training opportunities.** Most of the best training comes from the staff room. This is especially true if you have a friendly staff. Much of the talk in staff rooms seems to be about how teachers handle situations, how they tackle problems, how they teach different concepts and how they cope with a particularly difficult child. So take and use your coffee and lunch breaks and enjoy a good chat because it's not idle gossip – it's professional development.

18

Offering In-Service Training (INSET)

Most primary school teachers are now expected not only to be teachers but also to be 'curriculum experts'. As a 'curriculum expert' you may be asked to devise INSET or courses, or you may feel that you are competent to offer your colleagues training in your field of expertise. Further ideas about training are covered in the section 'Co-ordinating a curriculum area' but here we suggest some basic ideas which could prove helpful.

1 **Identify training needs for your curriculum area.** You can do this yourself, based on how you feel things are going in your subject or through a curriculum audit. However, probably the best and least threatening way is through the school development plan, if you have one. If so, get hold of it and see if your curriculum area is identified as needing attention as a whole, or in specific areas.

2 **Don't rush in!** Once you think you have established a training need, it might be tempting to go ahead and organise some INSET. However, it is well worth taking a step back and considering why this need has arisen. It could be that a lack of resources is more to blame, or it could be that there is a lack of progression and problems are being experienced because the ground work is not being undertaken effectively. Changes in staffing, sickness, unfamiliarity with resources, inconsistent interpretation of attainment targets and so on could be the source of the problem, and so training needs should be clarified at an early stage.

3 **Find out if there is someone better placed than you to help.** If the problem seems to be limited to a small number of staff or a single, isolated problem, you might be able to tackle it effectively by yourself, but if it is a more complex issue, why not ask if you can invite in your local education authority advisor or another qualified person to tackle the problem on your behalf?

4   **If you think you can do it yourself, don't get carried away**. Set yourself very specific and achievable targets. How much work you do to support staff in attaining those targets is up to you, but writing a specific brief and telling the staff what this is before you start helps to keep everything clearly focused. It also means that it is less likely that you will set up expectations that you cannot satisfy.

5   **If someone else (for example your headteacher) thinks you can do it yourself, ask them to help you set specific targets**. Once you have jointly established goals, it may be worth discussing their feasibility, and how you might go about tackling them in practice.

6   **Ask for time to get ready.** Arranging whole staff INSET is a very time-consuming job and many school managers will try to give their staff time to organise it. However, if the offer is not forthcoming, set out what you think you will have to do and approach your headteacher with your proposals. Once it is apparent what is involved, it is more likely that you will make your case to good effect.

7   **Keep notes on the INSET you provide.** Much of the INSET you offer will be one-to-one, because most of the time it's a question of you helping another teacher with a specific problem, especially if you have a specific area of curriculum responsibility. This sort of work tends to go unnoticed, so keep a note of what you have done as evidence of achievement in your own area of specialisation.

8   **If you keep getting individual requests about the same issues try to tackle the issue in a whole-staff group**. You might be in a position to offer a session that is more convenient to you, and it will be a more efficient use of your time if you can impart your pearls of wisdom to a collected audience.

9   **Don't expect to perform miracles.** When running INSET courses, it is tempting to try to provide really ambitious programmes, but taking on board a lot of new ideas in one go is hard. Providing notes and visual prompts on what you are talking about will help considerably. Many staff are happy if they just have something to take away with them that is well presented, provides useful guidance, and acts as a memory jogger. Try to break down areas for development into small, manageable steps.

10   **As far as possible, keep INSET sessions practical.** Listening to one person for an hour or so becomes boring. Practical activities tend to be easier to remember and often make more sense. Ensure that your INSET sessions are as well-planned, interactive and professional as your classroom teaching.

19

Communicating with colleagues

Effective communication can sometimes fall by the wayside in the rush of a school day, but it can also save a lot of wasted time. This set of tips addresses how you can keep one another informed, and keep up with what is going on, without getting bogged down in unimportant detail.

1   **Use the staff room notice board.** It is easy just to walk straight past but it can be a most effective communication tool if used well. Try moving things around and remove all the old notices, because a change makes a board more eye-catching. Use all of your creative display skills to draw attention to important information.

2   **Suggest to your colleagues that you should circulate a weekly diary.** This could let all staff know the main events of the week in advance. It helps to raise awareness about what is going on in the rest of the school, and helps colleagues to plan and coordinate activities effectively.

3   **Make the most of your opportunities at staff meetings.** They sometimes seem to be primarily forums for management to talk while teachers listen, but they are much more effective if used to keep one another informed. Take your chances at the end of the meeting, under 'Any other business' to circulate ideas or raise questions.

4   **Keep an eye out for local education authority advisory service network meetings.** These are run for curriculum coordinators and interested parties. They are a good opportunity to find out what is going on within your authority and collect good ideas that actually have been tried out and work in classrooms. You can also build useful networks of colleagues who are interested in the same kinds of areas as yourself.

5   **Take the ideas raised at network meetings back to your own school.** Many schools ask staff to report back on such meetings, but if you aren't required to but feel you have information worth sharing, you could put together an information sheet to circulate, or ask for a few minutes at the end of a staff meeting to give an oral report.

6   **Try to use appraisal as a communication opportunity.** Appraisal can seem a bit daunting, especially to new teachers but, if you prepare for it, it can be a positive developmental opportunity. Consider carefully what you would like to concentrate on and why. If there is an aspect of your work that you are unsure of, ask for this to be the focus of your appraisal. It is your responsibility to prioritise what will be looked at, so do not be afraid to take the lead.

7   **Keep careful notes about what you do as curriculum coordinator.** Reporting progress is likely to be part of your duties as a curriculum co-ordinator. Keep notes about requests you have received, action you have taken, resources you have ordered or organised and any other jobs you have undertaken. These will demonstrate what you have done and act as a good memory jogger for you and your colleagues.

8   **Try to keep a record of any dealings with outside agencies.** When communicating with services such as educational support services or equipment maintenance, make sure you keep a record of who you talk to, when you talked to them, how to get in touch with them, and what you discussed. This can be invaluable later on when follow-up action might be required.

9   **Start communicating with the schools into which your children will be moving.** Often this is simply a question of telling them what you think they want to know about the children they will be taking. Get them to write down what they want and when they want it. Ask for such details as early in the year as possible, to give yourself plenty of time to get all the information together. Try to establish a rapport with 'feeder schools' because there are bound to be things with which you can help one another.

10   **Keep minutes or action notes of all meetings.** Even if it is just a small sub-group meeting, it is still a good idea to keep a written record, however informal. Apart from anything else, it will remind everyone of what they agreed to, and what they promised to do.

20

Policies and schemes of work

Schools often have a surfeit of policy statements and schemes of work. Policies are put in place for good reasons, however, and it is as well to know what you need to know, and what responsibilities you have regarding policies and schemes of work. The following suggestions should help with this.

Policy statements for your curriculum area

1   **If the policy statement exists, check if it is up to date**. Many policy statements state how often they should be reviewed. It is important that a policy statement is relevant, recent, and read. It's pointless to work to a historic document.

2   **If the policy does not exist, check if you need to write one**. More often than not the answer will be yes! If it is, you will need to establish clear terms of reference, and make clear where the responsibilities lie for direction and implementation.

3   **Get hold of other policy statements.** They will give you the sorts of headings and statements that you need to put together your own policy. Schools sometimes have a 'house style' which you should adopt for your own statements too, without letting it be a straitjacket.

4   **Seek advice from your advisory service.** That is one of the things that it is there for. They should be able to tell you whether a draft statement covers all the areas that it should, or give you a skeleton policy statement and examples of good policy documents for you to emulate.

5   **Ask other colleagues within the authority.** Take your opportunities, either at network or pyramid meetings (other members of staff at your school might be able to help out here), to find examples of what others have found to be effective policies.

Schemes of work for your curriculum area

6   **Check that any scheme of work is the current version.** If not, it should still be fairly simple to update your scheme, but getting hold of other schemes, either from nearby schools or from the local education authority, might help you identify weaknesses or gaps within your own documentation.

7   **If there is no scheme, use your contacts to obtain sample schemes from elsewhere.** Find them from within the school or from the local education authority to give you a framework and headings to work from. You will, of course, need to customise any schemes you borrow for your own particular contexts.

8   **Remember that schemes of work should be dynamic.** This is especially important because they are rather complex documents. They should evolve from what is already going on in school. By comparing what is already going on with what you and the National Curriculum require, a scheme can be used to identify and fill gaps or weaknesses. But don't expect to produce one in a couple of days. Care taken at this stage will save problems from occurring later.

9   **If you want your scheme to work well, keep it straightforward.** It must be easy to use, easy to read and accessible. If teachers don't have a scheme to hand when planning activities, the chances are that they will ignore the process altogether and carry on doing it in the ways they are used to.

10   **Cut your coat according to your cloth.** It would be easy to think that once you have got a copy of someone else's scheme your problems will be entirely solved, but you have to tailor any scheme to the needs and the resources available in your school.

21

Making learning processes meaningful to children

One of the most important factors that can predetermine success in learning is confidence. It is important to give children every chance to gain this confidence and one of the best ways of helping them to do this is to help them to gain greater control over the processes they apply during their learning. These tips are designed to enable you to help children to make sense of how they are learning.

1 **Cultivate a desire to learn.** Children need to be motivated to learn things. They may need to be helped to increase their motivation by showing them what the benefits are. When possible, make learning fun, interesting and rewarding. Do not mistake lack of confidence for lack of motivation.

2 **Learning by doing is important.** Most learning happens when children practise things, have a go and learn by making mistakes and by finding out why. It is important to ensure that children are given early opportunities to try out and apply new things that they have been introduced to. There is no substitute for focused, practical experience.

3 **Feedback is essential.** Children need to find out how their learning is actually going. They may feel that they have understood something, but can't be certain until you let them know. Feedback must be well timed if it is to be of use to the child, and needs to be given to them in ways that they can readily understand and accept.

4 **Needing to learn something can be almost as productive as wanting to learn it.** When children know why something will be useful to them, even if they find it difficult, they are more likely to maintain their efforts until they succeed. Help them to understand the value of what they are doing, so they can make the most of the opportunity.

5   **Children need to try to make sense of what they are learning.** It is of little value learning things by rote, or becoming able to do things, without knowing why or how. It is also important that they have lots of opportunities to apply their new learning at an early stage. Putting things they have learned into practice helps them 'to get their heads round' the new ideas.

6   **Learning is not just a matter of storing up further knowledge.** Successful learning is about being able to use what has been learned, not just in familiar situations but also in new contexts. Help children to see how their learning can be transferable.

7   **Children take cues about how they are expected to learn from the ways in which we teach them.** If we concentrate on supplying them with information, they are likely simply to try and store it. If we structure our teaching so that they are practising, applying, extending, comparing and evaluating, they are more likely to see these processes as central to the ways in which they need to work.

8   **Learning is not just an independent activity.** While much can be learned by children working on their own with various learning resource materials, they can also learn a great deal by talking to each other and tackling tasks and activities jointly. Help them to gain benefit from working productively in pairs, threes and small groups.

9   **Becoming better at learning is important.** The most important learning outcomes in primary schools are not topic-based, but are the outcomes of being better able to learn new skills. Learning skills are among the most important of transferable life skills.

10   **Try to tune in to children's learning styles.** Sometimes children struggle because the way they are taught and the way they learn are in conflict. If you try different approaches to your classroom work, you are more likely to be able to keep some of the people happy all of the time. Some children will learn more from things they hear, others from things they see; some from tackling things alone, and others from working collaboratively. The more variety you can bring into the learning experiences you provide them with, the better each child's learning style will be accommodated.

22

Planning a new topic

Planning a new topic or unit of work from scratch can be a daunting task, but it can also be a rewarding experience, and a chance to enjoy the creativity that such a task involves. While you will still have to stick quite rigidly to curriculum guidelines, you can approach them in a wide variety of ways, using your initiative, and following your own interests – at least to some extent. However, you will need to ensure that your topic work integrates with the whole school plan and the National Curriculum requirements in order to avoid repetition and irrelevance. Here we offer a few practical guidelines, many of which are expanded upon elsewhere in this book.

1   **Clarify the key skills that the topic should cover.** You need to have a really clear idea about how you will ensure that the relevant key skills fit into your chosen topic. Check your other topics to see if you can identify gaps that you could try to tackle through your new topic.

2   **Identify basic concepts that could be covered by your topic.** These will be the 'meat on the bones' of your topic and will give it a subject focus, whether it is, for example, a scientifically or historically driven topic, or whatever the focus.

3   **Identify key questions that you want children to be able to answer**. These key questions will really be the starting points for the development of the skills and concepts identified above, and they will also provide you with the perfect assessment criteria. These will lead you naturally to the incorporation of the relevant learning outcomes, which you can identify by breaking down the basic concepts and key questions into simple steps. These learning outcomes can then shape the activities you will plan.

4   **Sort out what resources you will need.** Can most of your resourcing provision be found from inside school? Where could you go to get the resources you need? What visits/visitors could you arrange? Will other local education authority services be able to help? Will you be given any kind of budget?

5   **Decide upon a time-frame.** Although this may be dictated by existing arrangements, it is important to bear in mind the length of time you can afford to spend on a topic. You may be able to base this simply on how long you think you can sustain the children's interest, but other external factors, such as school events like sports days, open days, and school trips, can also impact on your plans and need to be taken into account.

6   **Consider the range of possible teaching and learning strategies.** Consider whether each activity will be most effectively tackled as a whole class, in small groups, or one-to-one. Consider whether each one should be tackled collaboratively or independently, with or without adult supervision and so on. Identifying these points at the planning stage might help you decide upon resources and timescales.

7   **Decide whether, and how, the learning outcomes might be assessed.** Much of your assessment will probably be continuous and informal, but some tasks may offer opportunities for more formal assessment, which you can build in to your overall assessment strategy.

8   **Consider the possibility of visits.** Do you know of any local sites suitable for field trips? Do any of your colleagues? Will the costs, in terms of time and money, make it worthwhile? Can you get out to have a look for yourself? How can you make sure that the visit will be a really worthwhile learning experience?

9   **Think about inviting in 'expert witnesses'.** If you are doing a historical topic, for example, asking grandparents or great-grandparents in to talk about their childhood can be very interesting for the children, and can bring the topic to life.

10 **Pick your best ideas as starting points and as conclusions.** Starting and finishing strongly gives a topic definition and purpose. An interesting visit to start with gives plenty of good ideas and motivation, a celebratory event, such as a teddy bears' picnic, at the end provides a good incentive.

Chapter 3   Pastoral Care

One of the most rewarding and demanding aspects of teaching young children is that you have an opportunity to build up a fairly close working relationship with a small number of children (relative to the numbers of children a secondary teacher may have to try to keep track of). Building this relationship can take a lot of time and effort and is an aspect of teaching that is difficult to teach anyone else to do. It is a very personal thing, but considering other people's approaches and points of view can help us tackle it in our own ways, with more confidence. Here we cover:

23   Dealing with upset children
24   Play times
25   Making children feel secure and comfortable
26   Helping children build self-esteem
27   Dealing with bad behaviour

23

Dealing with upset children

When working with young children, you are bound to have to deal with emotional upsets as there are any number of reasons why children might get themselves into states. How you deal with these situations is very much a personal thing and depends greatly on your experience of the child concerned, but possibly the most important thing is to calm the situation down quickly in order for you to get to the cause of the problem. These tips are designed to help you to take control of the situation promptly and effectively.

1 **Be firm, but gentle.** When children become upset, the most important thing is to get them settled as quickly as possible, so you can get to the bottom of it all. Telling them firmly that they need to calm down usually works more quickly than a lot of sympathy, which can inflame emotions further.

2 **Act quickly to settle children who don't want to be left at school by their parents or carers.** They may cling to whoever has brought them in. However, being firm usually sorts the problem out more quickly than prolonging the situation. Try telling the child exactly what they are going to do; more often than not in these cases children will do as they are told.

3 **If a child is upset, don't change your expectations.** If children think that they might get special favour or wriggle out of something they do not want to do just because they appear to be upset, then there is no incentive for them to calm down. Obviously, you have to be sensitive to the situation, but as a general rule, letting children off the hook does not help in the long run.

4 **If an upset child becomes disruptive, send for help.** If possible get another child to find help, in the shape of an auxiliary, nursery nurse or perhaps even the headteacher, because the child needs to be removed from the class to avoid disrupting the rest of the class. You may have to restrain the child to prevent harm to the child or others, but take extreme care never to use excessive physical force, which can never be condoned.

5 **Give a child time and space to calm down.** Sometimes getting upset might make children feel that they have lost face with the rest of the class. Giving them a little time and space by themselves affords them a chance to recover their composure and their dignity.

6 **Keep other children away.** A crowd is never conducive to getting an angry or distressed child to calm down; the sympathy seems to make them feel even more sorry for themselves. Again, it is a matter of being sensitive to the situation, but, generally, removing such children from the centre of attention helps them recover more quickly.

7 **Your experience of the children is the most important thing.** Knowing the children individually, the kinds of things they are interested in and what makes them laugh, can be very useful. Sometimes all that is required is that you distract children from the cause of their upset and get them to focus on something that is much more fun.

8 **Don't expect children to be able to explain why they are upset.** Sometimes they simply can't find the words to explain the way they feel. If children seem reluctant to talk about why they are upset or say they don't know why, it may simply be a matter of getting them calm and offering reassurance.

9 **If your discipline of children upsets them, don't let them get away with things for the sake of a quiet life.** Instead it can be a good idea to get them to sit quietly on their own and think about what they have done. This ensures that you have not climbed down but it also ensures that you do not end up upsetting the children further.

10 **Tell the children: 'You can tell me anything'.** Getting children to bring their problems to you, instead of bottling them up or dealing with them by themselves, is usually a good idea. This may make more work for you, but reassuring the children that you are on their side is important. Striking a balance between genuine support and perpetually sorting out petty disputes can be a bit tricky though. Nevertheless, it is important to provide opportunities for children to work through whatever concerns them, especially if it means you are alerted to serious problems which you may need to refer on for specialist help.

24

Play times

Supervising children at play times is part of most teachers' duties and is rarely, if ever, a dull affair. The potential for having a fistful of incidents all cropping up at once is high, but you still have to deal with them quickly and efficiently to make sure that things don't get out of hand. No teacher can expect to monitor everything that goes on, but these tips are designed to help you deal with play times to the best of your ability.

1 **Be clear in your own mind what is, and what is not, permitted**. Are the children allowed footballs or skipping ropes? Are they allowed on the field (if you have one)? If you do not know, you may open yourself up to a lot of persuasion and protest from the children. Ideally these decisions should be made by management and their decisions communicated to the children and to you. It is also useful if the lunch time supervisors know this to keep everything consistent.

2 **Check if there is a policy on the supervision of children at play time.** If there is, then it will probably give you guidance on how children are taken out of and brought back into school, on who should be available as back up (the designated first aider, for example), and on what to do in case of accidents (by way of recording incidents and informing parents or carers, and management) or who might supervise those children who have had play times suspended as a punishment.

3 **If there is no official policy, check if there is an unofficial one.** This information is useful because if your expectations are the same as the children's, it is all going to be much more straightforward. Check this out with the most established teachers in the school, who will normally be happy to share their wisdom with you.

4 **Once you know the rules of the game, stick to them!** Even if you disagree with some of the methods or procedures used, go along with them, because

dealing with a large number of children can be hard work. If you have concerns, raise them at a staff meeting and reach a consensus before making changes off your own bat.

5   **Try to enjoy yourself.** Play times tend to be less formal than classroom situations, and are good opportunities to get to know the children a little better, and for them to get to know you better too. While you are entitled to let your hair down a bit, make sure that you maintain your high expectations about how the children behave around and with you so as to avoid any misunderstanding. Excessive high spirits can spill over into classroom activities if you are not careful.

6   **Find out who could/should be on hand to help you when things go wrong.** You may have a great number of children to supervise, and you will not be able to attend to an injury or pursue someone who has decided they have had enough of school for the day. Make sure that you know who to send for as backup, and where they are likely to be, so that another child can be sent with a message.

7   **Check the local education authority's policies and practices before treating injuries yourself.** Most, if not all authorities, have clear guidelines on the treatment of injuries, including such things as the administration of a sticking plaster being done only by a designated first-aid trained member of staff. Make sure you know who this is, and if you are in any doubt about what you should do, just send for help.

8   **Buy your own whistle (if they are part of the school culture).** This is a wonderful way of gaining attention in a noisy playground. Keep it safe because, most certainly, someone will want to borrow it come play time and if there is a 'communal whistle', the chances are that the football coach will have borrowed it the previous night, and no-one will know where it is.

9   **Try not to overuse a whistle.** Children stop paying it any attention if it gets blown too often. Change your strategy by blowing the whistle, then using your voice to reinforce the whistle's command. Then praise good behaviour, single out bad behaviour, and you will probably achieve more impact than by repeated whistle blowing.

10 **Send your own class in from the playground last.** Otherwise they will find themselves unsupervised in an empty classroom. While they are with you they remain under your supervision; they may even see it as a kind of bonus.

25

Making children feel secure and comfortable

Children need to feel safe in your care. If you do not have their trust, getting them to make progress in your class is going to be an uphill struggle. It's not a question of wrapping them in cotton wool, however. Ideally you would want every child to feel comfortable in the classroom from day one, but building this relationship can take time with some children. Here are some ideas for you to establish the right kind of climate.

1   **Be consistent.** Treating all children the same way as consistently as possible is vital. If they know what to expect from you, and their expectations are justified, they will at least know where they stand, and that goes a long way to making them feel comfortable. Inconsistency is unfair to children, and lies at the root of a lot of poor behaviour, when children do not feel that they understand the rules of the game.

2   **Be fair.** This goes hand in hand with being consistent. In a busy classroom, it is all to easy to settle for an easy solution, but it is worth taking a step back and counting to ten. There will always be one or two children in the class who cause you more bother than all the rest, but they need to be dealt with fairly too if you are going to gain their trust. You may often, nevertheless, feel in need of the wisdom of Solomon!

3   **Remember that children often feel more comfortable in the presence of 'strict' teachers.** Although initially a firm teacher may be frightening, when the children discover that you are strict with those who do not do as they are asked, but perfectly lovely to those who get on and try hard, they will feel at ease. It's all about establishing clear boundaries.

4   **Children need to know that they can rely on you.** Most of all, they need to know that they can trust you to listen to what they have to say, and to help them to tackle their problems. Children need a lot of reminders about

this, and using anecdotes about how you have helped children in the past can help them to be assured of your trustworthiness.

5   **Children hate changes, and often find them unsettling.** Try not to move furniture or working groups around too often. Avoid changes in the timetable as far as possible, and take the time to explain when things do need to be changed. Many children begin to panic when things are not following their normal pattern. If major changes need to take place, for example, when buildings are refurbished, try to give the children as long as possible a lead time to prepare.

6   **Take your opportunities for reinforcing the idea that you are on their side.** If you have successfully dealt with a problem or concern, get the child concerned to tell the story of what happened and what was done about it. If it would embarrass them, then tell it on their behalf and anonymously. These stories help foster the idea that when things go wrong there is something that can be done.

7   **Make the classroom environment as reassuring as possible.** Cover the walls, because many children think that bare walls are scary. Putting up a bit of 'dazzle roll' or cheap wallpaper makes a classroom a much more inviting place. Try to get something interesting on the walls before introducing a new class to their new classroom.

8   **Try to give the children a space of their own.** A drawer and a peg to hang their coats, something they have ownership of, seems to be something of a touchstone for younger children. It can also be the source of argument and disruption, so you need to foster the idea that personal spaces such as work drawers are to be respected by others.

9   **Get down to their level.** When working with small children, they often seem to feel more comfortable when you are on their level, rather than physically, and possibly metaphorically, talking down to them. Making eye-contact will often be easier when you are sitting on a low chair, or kneeling beside them.

10 **Don't be excessively rigid**. Though you may have set clear guidelines about who certain children work with, or where they are expected to work, you may need to be flexible once in a while. However, you need to make sure this does not get out of hand. Try negotiating with the children so they get what they want in return for trying harder at something else. This way it isn't something they are likely to try to exploit.

26

Helping children to build self-esteem

Children who suffer badly from a lack of self-esteem often need a lot of support and fail to make good progress. Everyone needs a pat on the back once in a while, perhaps especially the really bright children. This does not have to be something that takes huge amounts of planning and preparation; it just takes a bit of thought and making the most of your opportunities.

1 **Give praise at every opportunity.** This will help not just the slower learners; everybody needs to be encouraged. Don't say something is good if it's not, however, as children seem able to see through this. If it *is* good, and the child concerned knows this is the case, then your praise has even greater impact.

2 **If your school has built-in reward systems, like 'show and tell' sessions, use them.** Keep a record of who takes work to show to the rest of the class, and try to keep a balance. Again, it means a lot more if everyone feels they have an equal chance. Try to ensure that the kinds of things that are celebrated are as diverse as possible, so it is not always the same ones who get the kudos.

3 **Consider whether ability grouping can help.** Children naturally compare themselves and their work to others in their class. If children are working with others of similar ability, then there is less likelihood that they will begin to worry about their own abilities. This way, everyone is likely to be kept reasonably happy.

4 **Put it on the wall.** Displaying a piece of work by mounting it and putting it on the wall can be an extremely good way of praising work and helping to build self-esteem. If you actually take the time and trouble to make a point of showing children's individual work on new displays, this could be the icing on the cake for them.

5   **As far as possible, make sure everyone gets something on to the wall.**
     This will ensure that all members of the class feel valued. Don't however,
     start to put up work that does not demonstrate at least a good effort,
     otherwise the children themselves might be highly critical of poor
     achievement.

6   **Differentiate tasks and activities to avoid frustration**. If tasks are chosen
     appropriate to the children's levels of ability, then the work they do will
     extend their abilities. However, avoid knocking their self-esteem by under-
     estimating their potential.

7   **Manage stressful situations.** When working on assessment tasks, the
     children may have to work independently. This can cause some to panic,
     so explain why you are getting them to work this way, and that you do
     not mind if their work is right or wrong, as long as they try their best and
     do their own work.

8   **Be straight, especially with the strugglers.** It is hard to be honest with
     them when work is not up to scratch simply because you want to be
     positive. Two things are important here. Firstly, that you say what you
     have to say without embarrassing the child: as far as possible, do it
     discreetly. Secondly, try to make sure that you end on a high note, for
     example using the tried and tested comment: 'I know you can do so much
     better!'

9   **Sometimes it is worth enlisting others' support.** If a piece of work
     represents a significant effort, and you want to take this opportunity to
     really encourage a child, you could let them choose to take the work to
     another teacher to show off. You may even be able to send them to the
     headteacher with good news.

10   **Pair or group children to facilitate success.** Sometimes getting a maths
     whizz-kid to work with someone who is struggling, or a technological
     genius to work with one who is all fingers and thumbs, can help both
     parties. The able children often benefit a lot, in terms of their own self-
     esteem, for being seen as an 'expert'. The less-able gain from the individual
     attention.

27

Dealing with bad behaviour

Dealing with bad behaviour is likely to be something you have to cope with day in and day out, or it may be something that fortunately only crops up from time to time. Either way, it needs to be handled firmly, confidently and consistently.

1   **Start with your school's policy on behaviour.** Knowing what procedures are in place and are supported by the school management will help you deal with bad behaviour consistently and positively. It is important for everyone in the school to sing to the same song sheet.

2   **Make sure there is consistency between teachers on what is, and what is not, acceptable.** Even disruptive and badly behaved children know the difference between a teacher who chops and changes, and one who always handles things firmly and fairly, and they respond accordingly. If they think there is a chance of getting a different reaction, they might try to provoke one.

3   **Keep the class informed when disruption occurs.** It can be useful to tell the rest of the class exactly what has taken place, although care should be taken not to embarrass the child concerned unduly. This serves two purposes: firstly, to reinforce the consequences of poor behaviour, and secondly, to stop gossip running rife, which could prolong the discomfort of the child concerned.

4   **Avoid open confrontation as far as possible.** It could be that children will become distressed or even violent when faced with having to deal with the consequences of their own behaviour. They may feel threatened and foolish, and being given the time out to draw back from the brink is usually a good idea.

5   **You can say an awful lot with body language.** Often that is all that is required to avert potentially disruptive behaviour. A look, a raised eyebrow or a gesture can remind children of what is expected of them without making a big deal of it. Experienced teachers learn a range of non-verbal language to communicate effectively with naughty children.

6   **Never issue an ultimatum that you cannot stand by.** If you warn a child that you will do something, and then do not do it, you will lose your credibility and inflame the situation further.

7   **Use different voices for different circumstances.** The tone of your voice may well say a lot more than the words you are speaking. Your voice can express a wide range of emotions, and this can influence children's behaviour profoundly. Children seem to respond more to the way in which something is said than to *what* is said.

8   **Don't always blame yourself.** If a child behaves badly in class, there is often an underlying reason that has nothing to do with your expertise in managing behaviour in the classroom. Recognise that children behave badly for all kinds of reasons, and it is not always in your power to influence the causes of such behaviour.

9   **If a problem continues, seek support.** If a child's behaviour becomes too disruptive over a considerable period of time, remember that it is not just your problem. Approach your headteacher, special needs coordinator or mentor about how this bad behaviour could be managed more effectively.

10   **Remember your responsibility to yourself.** If persistent bad behaviour is getting you down, approach your headteacher or someone who can help you manage the situation professionally. You should not feel that you have to cope alone.

Chapter 4   Making and Managing Resources

Primary teaching often seems to be a very resource-driven task. Producing stimulating, relevant and beneficial aids to help you teach is obviously essential, but can also become extremely time-consuming and is not necessarily the key to being a good teacher. The most important resources in your classroom are you and your experience, but having the right teaching and learning aids to hand will make you a more efficient and confident teacher. This chapter aims to give ideas about what is worth doing, how to do it efficiently and how to use it to its best advantage.

28

Obtaining resources

All schools have a wide variety of resources that might help you in your teaching and in the management of your class. Finding out what they have and where they are stored is another matter. You may find much of what you need, but you will probably have to make or borrow some of it for yourself.

1   **If you are new to a school, try to get in before school starts.** It is always a good idea to try to get into school well before the beginning of term and have a look through resource rooms and cupboards in your classroom. Keep a note of the resources that you think might come in useful, and start thinking how you can use or adapt them for your own purposes.

2   **Review the topics that you will be teaching, and what you need to do about planning for those topics.** This will give you a much better idea of what resources you might need, making any lists of available resources you keep even more useful. You can then quickly locate and use material that is immediately relevant and useful.

3   **Try to consider the resources you will need for the other work you might cover.** Think about what you might be dealing with in number, practical maths, phonics, technology, science and so on. See if you can collect resources for these subjects to kit out your classroom before you need it all.

4   **Learn how to laminate your paper resources.** If you make any work cards, get them laminated or 'Shire Sealed' to protect them from the rigours of classroom life. Even sealing master copies of worksheets that you intend to photocopy is a good idea, as they tend not to get dog-eared so quickly. Colleagues and children are also more likely to return laminated resources than paper sheets.

5   **Store master copies of work sheets in plastic wallets.** If your school does not have them, then buying them in boxes of 100 from office supplies stores is fairly cheap to do. Storing sheets in special files for different subjects or topics is a good idea too. The better you index your materials, the less time you will spend hunting for them.

6   **Using work cards can save on photocopying.** They allow you to give children slightly different tasks, cutting down on copying in class too. However, they take a lot of time and effort to make, so preserve the investment by keeping master copies and photocopy the master on to card. Keep the master copy in a safe (separate) place, just in case.

7   **Try to share resources.** If you work in a two- or three-form entry school, it is likely that you and your year group colleagues will be duplicating resources. Get together and plan who will produce what and cut the time you spend on making resources in half (or double the number of resources you can produce).You might also be able to borrow resources, or a least glean good ideas from teachers who have worked in your year group in previous years.

8   **Bear in mind that preparing too far in advance might be counter productive.** It is tempting to use a summer holiday to get prepared for the whole year, but producing or collecting resources too far in advance can be a waste of time, because you might find that they are inappropriate or even irrelevant, especially if you are relatively new. You may need to spend a little time tuning in to what the children in a new class need.

9   **Buying a computer with a reasonable printer for home use, will save you huge amounts of time in the long run.** Making multiple versions of slightly varying resources is so much easier when you don't have to start from scratch each time, and this is what computers are good at! It is also advantageous to be able to work at your own pace and when you feel like it, rather than having to do everything on the school premises.

10 **The very best resources are the ones that can be used flexibly in many different ways.** Blank 100 Squares, number spirals, number squares, alphabet ladders, letter and number cards are worth their weight in gold because they can be used in so many different ways. Building up stocks of these sorts of resources can prove useful over and over again.

29

Choosing and using printed learning resources

The array of printed resources available to children in school can be bewildering. Children need to be helped (or taught) to use these resources effectively and you will need to make sure that the resources are well managed and maintained so as to get the best out of them.

1   **Identify the intended learning outcome from each resource.** Many learning packages already contain explicit learning objectives, but you may need to customise these, depending on the context of your topic and on the abilities of your children. Being very clear about what you want to achieve with learning resources is crucial to success.

2   **Plan in advance what you might be intending to assess.** Will you be able to use the materials you have chosen to inform your planning and to fulfil assessment tasks? Make sure that you tailor assessments to the identified goals you have set yourself, to give your children the best possible opportunities to show their best work in assessed tasks.

3   **Give children the chance to develop appropriate self-help skills.** Different resources can be used to develop different approaches, especially if they are accessible and well displayed. Give responsibility where you can to children to select and use resources in a variety of ways.

4   **Try to strike a balance between independent and collaborative work.** There are considerable advantages in planning work in small groups, especially when resources and materials are limited. However, being able to work independently is important, not least for assessment of each child's understanding. Ideally, use learning resources to give children the chance to work both cooperatively and independently.

5   **Help children to put the skills they gain into a context.** It helps children if they know why the things they are learning will be of value to them. For example, being able to find a book at school has relevance regarding how to use libraries outside. Being able to use the contents page will help them find what they are looking for quickly and is an invaluable skill. Being able to load a computer programme at school has relevance at home and perhaps later in their working lives.

6   **Try to find out how well materials have already worked elsewhere.** Try to get feedback from other teachers. Ask them whether they were really worth the money. Did they help cut down the work load? Did they help with assessment? Did they remain current, or did they start to date quickly? Did the children enjoy using them?

7   **Consider whether the materials will be self-supporting and self-sufficient.** Some learning packages rely on the availability of other resources, such as textbooks, others do not. Before you purchase them, it is worth asking whether you have sufficient, or if further resources are required.

8   **Look for materials that can be freely copied.** Photocopied materials can work out cheaper than a one-off learning package. Be very careful to ensure that you do not infringe copyright, as legislation is quite strict in this domain.

9   **Be aware of 'apparent' quality.** Some materials look impressive, but it is more important that the actual learning opportunities are sound and relevant. 'All that glisters is not gold' – glossy production can sometimes be used to mask poorly thought-out learning materials.

10   **Monitor children's learning from resources.** Do they find it easy to use them effectively? Do they enjoy using them? Do they affect the quality of their work? Are they eager to work with them, or are they reluctant to use them? If you do discover that you have purchased something that children hate, it is as well to cut your losses rather than persevere with materials that are plainly unsuitable.

30

Deciding on what is most important for you to do

Simply because there will never be enough time to do all the things that you might want to do, it is important that you prioritise your jobs. Sometimes it is obvious what must be done first, especially in the short term, but planning ahead and prioritising your work well in advance will help you avoid wasting valuable time.

1   **Remember that you are the most valuable resource in your classroom**. Your first responsibility is to yourself because you are the person who keeps your classroom running smoothly. Make time for yourself, and consider your own needs as well as those of the children.

2   **At the end of a school day, first relax, then tidy up.** Perhaps get yourself a cup of tea and then set the classroom straight. It is amazing how much better things look when you know your classroom is sorted out and your records are up to date. It is also easy to feel that there are more important things to do first, but if you neglect your classroom then it is likely that the children will too. Avoid as far as possible leaving it all to the next day, when other priorities are likely to impinge.

3   **Get the most immediate things done first.** If you can develop the discipline of getting your paperwork sorted out before you do anything else, then you know that you can afford to devote whatever time there is left in the day to less immediate things.

4   **Remember that making absolutely perfect resources for tomorrow's lesson might be unachievable.** Having well-presented, immaculate worksheets is a target to strive for, and they are always nice to have, but remember that *you* do the teaching, not the worksheet. It is better to compromise with reasonable quality than to struggle for perfection to the point of exhaustion.

5   **Recognise that making good resources for the next day's lesson might save you a lot of time.** They can help you to use your time in the classroom more effectively because children will have a better chance of using them unaided, allowing you more time to focus on what you want to do. Use the time you have available to make the most of what you have.

6   **Use your record keeping and planning to help prioritise essential jobs.** At the topic planning stage, it might be a good idea to make a list of resources you think you will need and to decide roughly when you will need them. If you have any spare time or a willing helper, working through the list might help you actually get ahead of yourself.

7   **At the topic planning stage, get hold of catalogues as well as resource books.** They will give you lots of good ideas and identify useful resources you might need, well ahead of time, so you can order them in advance. If you are really organised you can also submit requisitions and get photocopying done in advance.

8   **Plan in advance to make the best of opportunities to beautify your classroom.** Again, at the planning stage, make a list of displays and activities that you would like to have in your classroom. Order, collect or scrounge what you are likely to need for them. This means that you will never be stuck to know what to do next and that you will always have a list of jobs ready for any additional help you might be offered.

9   **Consider what are the best uses of your time.** You may sometimes have to decide between keeping your paperwork and records up to date, or preparing resources for the next lesson. It is a difficult balancing act, but often short term priorities will have to win, for pragmatic reasons.

10 **Recognise that you cannot achieve everything that you might wish to do.** You may, for example, want to reorganise and label the resources by the water tray, or set up an interactive display for number investigation. However, you need to accept that such activities as these, although they are an important part of making your classroom a stimulating place to learn, are luxuries rather than essentials.

31

Identifying and filling in the gaps

Whether you are working in a school that has meticulous planning and record-keeping procedures, or one that barely offers any guidance at all, you will still come across gaps in provision of National Curriculum requirements, resources, guidance, your area of responsibility and in your classroom work. Identifying and filling in those gaps is a long process, but will help you ensure that you do your job properly.

1   **In long-term planning, cross-reference activities with learning out-comes**. If you are working with existing planning guidelines, photocopy the guidance notes and keep them in a prominent place. Tick off the learning outcomes as you plan an activity that covers them. This will help you to monitor continuously what you are achieving.

2   **In short-term planning, cross-reference actual work with planned work.** Keep an additional photocopy of your planning sheets and tick off each activity as you do it. This way you avoid creating gaps in the first place. It also gives you a great sense of personal satisfaction, as the sheets get progressively busier.

3   **In planning for your curriculum area, cross-reference planned outcomes against National Curriculum requirements.** If you are planning or reviewing the provision for your curriculum area, get a copy of the programme of study from the National Curriculum, and tick off each part as you identify it within the whole school plan.

4   **Nothing beats effective record keeping**. If your records are thorough and up to date, identifying the gaps will be so much easier. If there is a system for record keeping in your school, use it. If not, make your own: it is not just a matter of being well-prepared for OFSTED inspections, it is part of being a professional.

5   **When trying to plug the gaps, use every other source possible.** If you have identified a gap in provision whilst reviewing your curriculum area, look through source books, catalogues, the library, and talk to colleagues and other staff concerned for ideas on how they cover these areas.

6   **Consult the rest of the staff when planning changes that are to be made.** If, having completed a review of provision for your curriculum area, you identify gaps in provision and need to add to existing plans, it is essential to approach the staff concerned with some ideas, and the paperwork that shows where the gap exists, before making any firm decisions. By involving them in the decision making, you are more likely to bring them along with you in any changes you initiate.

7   **Try bringing up issues in the staff room.** The biggest database of ideas that will help you fill gaps in your planning is the experience of the rest of the staff, and 99 times out of 100 someone will have tackled the problem before. Use your colleagues as a resource, to help you to bridge gaps, rectify omissions, and correct for oversights.

8   **Approach the subject coordinator for assistance.** If you come across a gap in provision that you don't feel you have the expertise to fill as effectively as you should, ask the subject coordinator. Such colleagues might not always be able to help, but they should be able to put you in touch with someone who can.

9   **Use your local education authority advisory service.** Although they are usually only available for assistance with school-wide issues, they can help you to ensure that the provision in your school is complete, and can help with ideas and resources to remedy deficiencies. They also have a wealth of expertise and experience you can draw on.

10   **Map basic skills across the curriculum.** Whilst mapping skills progression across the whole school and the whole curriculum is a highly complex task, breaking it down into Key Stages, or even year groups, can make it more manageable, and can give guidance to staff and help to ensure continuity of provision.

32

Using other people to produce classroom resources

See also 'Using other adults in the classroom' in Chapter 1. If you have access to parents, governors or members of the community who are willing to help, do at least consider the opportunity. Be aware also that some people who would like to help cannot give time to work in the classroom, but may be able to offer support in the production of classroom resources.

1   **Cast your net wide.** Sometimes people are reluctant to come forward and offer help, so send out a letter or put up posters, making it clear that there are many ways in which people can assist. These do not necessarily involve working alongside you in the classroom.

2   **Use positive influence to get assistance whenever possible.** If you are trying to press-gang a few into helping out, foster the idea that the school can only work well with help from the community. Point out that even someone with just a half an hour to spare can be of use. Foster a sense that children's learning is the responsibility of everyone concerned, not just that of teachers.

3   **Give helpers an example of what you want.** If you are getting others to make or prepare resources for you, it is often easier to show them rather than to explain what is required. It may also give them confidence to watch what you do, and to practise while you are there to give them feedback (and lots of praise and thanks).

4   **Only provide sufficient resources to complete the task.** With the best will in the world, helpers often forget how precious and limited school resources are. Making sure that you give the right amount of resources will help preserve stocks and make your requirements clear.

5   **Be realistic about setting time goals.** Both in and out of the classroom, giving people a clear idea of how long it should all take will help ensure that the task is done in the way you want. Some people offering help might otherwise strive to achieve unrealistically high levels of perfection, and then become fed up, ultimately withdrawing their support.

6   **Train your helpers to be aware of everyday chores.** You might want to draw up a list of jobs linked to learning resources that are always in need of attention, such as sharpening pencils, cleaning paint pots, sorting shelves, tidying and cataloguing resources, and so on. This way you will be able to make the best use of helpers' time.

7   **Ask helpers to *support* the children in management of resources.** Children need to learn not to waste resources unnecessarily, and to tidy up after themselves. Classroom helpers can reinforce this.

8   **Try not to depend excessively on voluntary help.** Sometimes it will not become apparent until the eleventh hour that the help you had expected is not going to materialise. When you plan activities that will rely on such help, spare a thought for what will happen if you are let down. Have contingency plans to cope with the situation.

9   **Get volunteers to keep their eyes open.** If you keep parents and helpers up to date with what is happening in the classroom, they can keep an eye out for materials and resources that might come in useful, or offer suggestions for valuable, additional opportunities to extend your work. External people often have access to all kinds of free or cheap materials that can supplement your restricted stock.

10 **Consider sending jobs home.** Some parents or volunteers might be able to tackle jobs such as sewing, mounting work, laminating or 'Shire Sealing' work cards or books better at home than in the classroom. Make sure, however, that you let them know if the job is urgent!

33

Access to resources

Life in the classroom tends to be happier and more productive if the children know where to find things, and if they access what they need when they need it. How you set up and manage this will depend on facilities you have available, and what options you have about where and how it is stored. The following suggestions give some general principles you may bear in mind, to make life easier for yourself.

1   **Put as much as possible out on show where the children can see it.** You may have shelving in your classroom that will help you display the resources that you have, but you might need to resort to taking cupboard doors off fixed units to give you more accessible shelf space.

2   **Organise resources according to curriculum areas.** It makes sense to collect resources for one subject in one area. Materials can be further categorised by having resources specifically, for example, for number work or supporting written work, grouped separately.

3   **Have your categories clearly identified.** If you colour-code the containers in which you keep your resources according to the subject that they support, it will be easier for the children to work out where resources should be put back, and what kinds of work they are likely to be used for.

4   **'Shadow' and label your shelves.** If every resource container is clearly labelled with the name of what should be placed there, clearly marked in the space from which it came, children will know what to put where. If your shelves are 'shadowed' and labelled they will know where resources should go, but most importantly, you will be able to see precisely what is missing when tidying up has not been done properly.

5   **Use pictorial cues where possible.** Labels and shadow labels may not help if children can't read. Providing visual cues to the contents of containers or shelves, as well as the relevant title will support those with poor reading skills, and may help reinforce useful vocabulary.

6 **Draw the children's attention to what is available.** It is easy to assume that, just because things are on display, the children will know where they are. Point out to them what is there for their use. Discuss why it is sorted and stored in the way that it is. Ask them what they think those particular resources might be for.

7 **Collect and display resources for investigation.** Getting children to think about investigation, and raise questions, isn't always easy. Having interesting resources out on show for them to explore, discuss, handle and look at may provide opportunities for exactly that.

8 **Do not expect role-play areas to run themselves.** Providing a beautiful home corner, or an exquisite post office for the children to play in, is not enough in itself. If you don't have time to play in there too, talk to the children about what things are for, what they could do, read relevant stories, show videos, indeed use anything you can to give them ideas to try out in their play.

9 **Put resources at child height.** If the children cannot see resources left out on shelves or in cupboards, because they are too high up, it will rarely occur to them to try and use them. Worse still, they may get into danger if they try to climb up to get them down.

10 **Label things that cannot readily be looked into.** If resources that are stored in plastic boxes or cupboards are for the children to use, then label them clearly and, if possible, put some kind of visual clue on the front too. This will help to draw things to their attention and possibly to stimulate their interest.

34

Accessing materials and resources outside school

Resources, materials and support are widely available if you know where to look and you are not afraid to ask. Some sources will be linked to your local education authority and others will be private ventures. All are worth plundering in order to stock your classroom and enhance your curriculum.

1   **Remember that local shops are worth a visit.** Some companies set aside an amount of stock to donate to schools and charities. Asking for raffle prizes or tombola supplies can take time, but can also be rewarding. It is amazing what people can give you for free, if you are cheeky enough to ask. Make sure you speak to the managers or supervisors, however, who usually have authority to write off stock. Junior staff may just dismiss your request out of hand, because they do not know company policy or are not authorised to made decisions of this sort.

2   **Don't be afraid of your computer.** Most authorities have a technology development and support centre. They will be able to advise you about hardware and software, and will usually have hardware for you to try out on loan. They also may be able to advise you about how to get hold of equipment that has been declared superfluous or redundant, but which may be just right for your needs.

3   **Plunder schools library services to boost topic resources**. You are likely to be able to borrow from a wide range of project collections which usually include maps, posters and booklets as well as books. This can extend the stock of resources you have in school, and can provide a greater variety of materials for you and your children.

4   **See if you can borrow things from local museums.** Many museums have education departments that will lend objects to schools, or staff to bring objects into school and talk about them. Obviously, you will need to take care of whatever is loaned to you, but children are often stimulated and excited by real artefacts.

5   **Find out if you have a multicultural resource centre.** Centres can provide resources as well as offer training courses. They are likely to offer specialist services and materials, which will extend your repertoire and provide valuable diversity in the classroom.

6   **Try to get experts into school.** You may be able to persuade parents or people from local religious and social groups to visit the school and talk to the children. They will need briefing carefully about the level of the work done by the children they are working with, and what you hope to achieve, but the benefit to all parties is likely to be high. Visitors enhance credibility.

7   **Take opportunities to work with others who teach in the same age range as you.** Many Local Education Authorities run, for example, 'Early Years' meetings where you can meet regularly to discuss planning and working styles and share ideas with other schools around you. These can provide invaluable networking opportunities, and may help you to feel less alone in your work if you are new to the job.

8   **Find out about local resource centres.** Many councils bring together under one roof a variety of resources and materials that have been donated from other areas of the council and businesses. It is amazing what a treasure-trove you can often access in this way.

9   **Do not be afraid to beg, scrounge and plead.** Local businesses, whose raw materials could be of use to you, can often be persuaded to provide materials free of charge, as long as you will take what you are given and collect it yourself. What are, to them, often waste materials, such as off-cuts, roll-ends, and so on, can provide super materials for the classroom. Take special care, however, that what you bring into your school is safe for children to use.

10 **Try to visit jumble sales and car boot sales.** Or get a parent or helper to go for you. It is amazing how many costumes and props you can find for next to nothing. You will, of course, need to check everything carefully, to make sure it is clean, serviceable and safe. You might also need to live with sympathetic people who can cope with your need to hoard all kinds of junk!

Chapter 5 Assessment and Record Keeping

Effective assessment and record keeping are essential for effective teaching. Without good and consistent assessment of your pupils' abilities, you can't plan or provide work that moves the children on at the right rate. Similarly, without efficient and effective record keeping, you can't be sure that your pupils are progressing as well as they should. This chapter offers some practical suggestions about how to do both, without them becoming too much of a chore.

35

Keeping track of progress

Keeping your records and documentation in order will help you to keep track of many of the things that go on in a busy classroom, both in the long and short term. They are useful not only in terms of good management, but also in terms of demonstrating to other interested parties what is going on. Tracking progress should be a part of whole school policy.

1   **Think about how best to use matrices and tick sheets.** Draw up a list of the names of the children in your class against a blank grid, and then photocopy it several times. This sort of grid can be used in any number of ways and situations to record vital information.

2   **Keep records of each child's individual activities, as well as of those of the class as a whole.** Tick sheets can give a good overview of what is going on in a classroom if used to record and plan the tasks the children have undertaken, and can provide a record of what they have achieved. You can also then keep track of each child's progress in important areas.

3   **Use tick sheets as an assessment tool.** Each activity described on your matrix will have a learning outcome identified in your planning. Use them to record whether you feel that each individual has actually understood what has been done. It will also help you to build evidence of individual achievement for formative assessment.

4   **Get advice on keeping formal recording procedures.** Many schools will have some form of standardised record keeping and assessment. Seek advice from a mentor or appropriate coordinator on how to use them and try to get ideas about how different people use them and keep them up to date. Sometimes the job is not as onerous as it first seems.

5   **Keep your records as simple as possible.** If you are not required to keep records of individuals' achievements against National Curriculum targets, but feel it would be useful, simply photocopy relevant pages from the National Curriculum documentation and highlight those aspects of the level descriptions a child has attained. This will provide you with a clear overview of achievement.

6   **Identify opportunities for assessment as you go.** You can use any and every task as an assessment task, if it seems appropriate and sensible. If you always decide what you want the children to learn before you decide the activity you are going to use to teach it, you will automatically have identified what it is that you could assess through that work.

7   **Manage your class in such a way that you have time to spend with every child.** Keeping track of what everyone in the class is doing is very tricky, especially if you are running an integrated day. Concentrate on one job at a time and train the children to expect that you will be there to support them at all times, but that you will share your time out between them. This helps prevent you from being interrupted, unless it is an emergency. Get the children used to the idea that normally you will approach them, rather than vice versa.

8   **Use the observations of helpers in your class.** If auxiliaries or parents have been well briefed about activities that are undertaken with groups of children, they will know what you are looking for and their observations and comments will be useful in helping you to monitor activities and achievements.

9   **Get the children to do some of the recording for you.** Older children should be well able to take responsibility for recording what they have achieved in class, so they could fill in record sheets for you. With younger children the same thing could be achieved, but will require an imaginative approach. You could, for example, ask them to put stickers on to a wall chart once they have completed a task, which has a specific outcome which you could review later.

10 **Grow eyes in the back of your head.** Or at least try to tune in to the more unusual sounds or movements in the classroom. If they are unusual, then they probably should not be happening. The price of peace is eternal vigilance.

36

Assessment and planning

The ideal situation in the organisation of your teaching is that you should teach what the children need to know, find out if they have understood it or not and then continue to the next area. This link between planning and assessment can be tricky to establish, so you need to adopt systematic structures to ensure that such connections are established.

1   **Don't be afraid to use your intuition.** One of the most useful forms of assessment is the impression you build up about the children in your class, what their needs are and where they are going. Such informal assessment, however, should be supplemented by evidence of achievement, as described in the section on 'Keeping track of progress', to avoid subjectivity swaying your judgement.

2   **Don't be afraid of going over the same ground.** Children cannot be relied upon to learn in a developmental way. If you feel that a child has not grasped an idea, giving the same task presented in a different way will be valid and valuable reinforcement. Classroom assessment should never be a 'sudden death' situation, where only one attempt is permitted.

3   **Don't reinvent the wheel.** There are plenty of good ideas for assessment opportunities and planning strategies in source books and magazines. If they suit your purpose, use them; if they are not a perfect match, just adapt them. Creative recycling is an excellent pedagogical principle!

4   **Try to keep planning for topic work and core skills separate.** If you tie core skills to topic planning, you might find that progress through the topic dictates progress through core skills. It should be your informal assessment of progress in these skills that determines what happens next.

5   **Don't underestimate the value of formal assessment as a record of achievement.** Although formal assessment may not appear to help you to plan and teach, it is a good way of charting children's progress and identifying trends that may indicate problems. It may also provide base line data upon which you can make comparisons.

6   **Don't over-estimate the value of formal assessment in assisting planning.** Many schools undertake a programme of formal assessment over and above those that are statutorily required. While, in theory, these assessments should assist you in your planning, in reality they often only serve to confirm your expectations. When the findings do not ring true with your gut feelings, take them with a pinch of salt, while keeping an open mind about whether your hunches might have been wrong.

7   **Keep formal assessment manageable.** When carrying out formal assessment tasks, try to make them as similar as possible to those relating to ordinary classroom situations. It is probably better to annotate a piece of work outlining how it was completed, and then take this into account when grading it, than to force children to do it under 'exam conditions' where they might perform very badly.

8   **Remember that planning may need to be flexible.** If your assessments indicate that your long-term planning was over optimistic, or is not stretching the children enough, make a note of it and go with what your observations indicate to be a most useful course of action. All action planning should be dynamic and responsive to changing situations, otherwise it becomes merely an exercise.

9   **Ask questions.** Conversations with children about the work that they have been doing may reveal far more about their understanding of this work than a formal test. Their responses to questions can reveal whether a piece of good work is mainly due to a good comprehension of the concept or task, or due to a lucky guess.

10 **Try to remember that the most under-used question is 'Why?'** If children are able to explain what they have done, and why they have done it, it is a sure sign that they understand the concept well.

37

Learning outcomes

Writing learning outcomes provides a systematic way of planning how required elements of the curriculum will be delivered and evaluated. More teachers have to justify what they are planning to do in terms of what children will learn, and how they intend to assess whether that outcome has been understood. However, many people do find learning outcomes hard to come to terms with, so these tips are designed to smooth the way.

1   **Start from what you hope your children would be able to achieve by the end of a unit of work.** You may well be working with a topic that is already planned in terms of objectives or outcomes, but it is worth thinking about your goals for each session and how these will be achieved. If everything went absolutely to plan, what would the ultimate outcomes be like? Then you can start planning how to get there.

2   **Remember the difference between an aim and an objective.** An aim is a long-term goal that may take several weeks or even a term to fulfil. This is usually achieved by breaking the aim down into a series of short-term, specific objectives and working through them. So an aim might be 'To develop children's familiarity with traditional stories', and linked objectives might be 'To listen to the story of ...', 'Sequence the main events in the story of...' and so on.

3   **Express learning outcomes in terms of actions.** Use lively action verbs such as: 'be able to...', 'Know the difference between...', 'Know why...', or 'Respond appropriately to...', and so on, to demonstrate exactly what it is that the children are expected to become able to do.

4   **Work out how children will demonstrate their understanding.** Will this be through discussion, filling in a work sheet, a tally or pro forma, through written work, charts or diagrams or simply getting the answer right in a classroom task? If you are clear about the evidence that you require to demonstrate achievement, the children will be too.

5　**Be selective about the evidence of achievement that you require.** You might be able to think of several ways a child could demonstrate understanding, but pick the one that you think will be the most appropriate, and stick to just that single activity. This will make it easier for you to manage, and will prevent children being overwhelmed by assessment requirements.

6　**Decide what constitutes comprehension and what does not.** Your learning outcome may not contain quite enough information to act as a strict guide to assessment. Consider whether 'eight out of ten' is enough or whether, to demonstrate proficiency, children need to get everything right.

7　**Keep learning outcomes specific and very short term.** Units of work can usually be broken down into specific outcomes. These can often be tackled by having one outcome taught through one activity in one session. Outcomes should never be multiple, vague, or internally contradictory.

8　**Consider whether one task might be able to assess many outcomes.** Combining assessments in this way will keep the work more manageable for you, and more interesting for the children. You will probably find that developing integrative assessment tasks is really productive and creative.

9　**Don't be afraid of using the same outcome more than once.** Many aspects of classroom work have to be repetitive to be effective, and so when a learning outcome is particularly important, it is likely to recur in a variety of different guises.

10　**Keep the language of learning outcomes simple.** Don't feel that you need to dress them up in complex vocabulary: write outcomes that are clearly understandable by your colleagues, support staff, volunteers, helpers, and ideally, by the children themselves.

38

National Curriculum assessment

In the UK there are nationally standardised curriculum descriptors for schools, which outline what should be taught and assessed in all state schools. Feelings about these are mixed, but they have become part of every state school teacher's working life. These tips are designed to make National Curriculum assessment tasks of greatest possible benefit to you and to your children.

1   **Have faith in your own experience.** Almost inevitably there are going to be times when children either under- or over-perform in national tests. Do not feel undermined by these results if you disagree with what they suggest. All kinds of factors impinge on children's achievements in formal tests, and they do not always perform to your expectations, or to their own potential.

2   **Have faith in the children.** The chances are that they will know something unusual is going on when taking an important assessment. It might be best to tell them exactly what is going on, without overplaying the test's importance. Children will not be fooled if you just pretend that nothing special is happening.

3   **Consider the possibility that the children might actually enjoy the experience.** Sometimes the novelty value of a situation can make it a positive experience for the children. Try playing on this and make it an occasion: special pencils, new erasers, a new room and so on.

4   **Don't feel that coaching in 'exam technique' is cheating.** In fact, to give children a fair chance, they will do better in the tests if you introduce ideas such as timed written work, or discussion of the possible interpretations of a maths problem. Rehearsal opportunities in stress-free contexts will help them to get used to what is expected of them, and may lead to better performance. However, do not let preparation for tests take over the life of the classroom.

5 **Try to get yourself trained.** Many education authorities offer support and training for staff undertaking Standard Assessment Tasks (SATs). Even if you have used SATs before, you might benefit from such an opportunity to learn more about the tests, and how they impact on children.

6 **Try a couple of dummy runs.** It takes a little while for teachers to understand the format and required procedures for certain tasks in Key Stage One SATs. You could try out the process on a couple of children who will not be assessed that year, say from another class, in advance of giving the tests to your own class, so that if you get muddled or confused, it will not affect the performance of the children when it really matters.

7 **Get hold of past papers.** You do not have to use them under test conditions, but try including them as normal classroom activities. You will have opportunities to help children to think their way through the problems they encounter and they will get used to the format of the papers.

8 **With one-to-one tests, leave your lower attainers until last.** Some of the tests are spread out over a number of weeks. Leaving your lower attainers until last might give them a little more time, to make the difference between one level and another.

9 **Encourage children to 'have a go' at questions that they find difficult.** The more you can encourage the idea that a guess is better than no answer at all, the better the children's chances of picking up the odd additional mark. Sometimes children can be fearful of looking silly, so may keep quiet rather than risking a wrong answer.

10 **Keep parents or carers informed.** Once times and dates are confirmed for testing procedures, it can be helpful to pass this information on to parents or carers. They are bound to be curious and will want to know what is going on. It will also give you the opportunity to explain the school perspective, and hopefully avoid rumours getting out of control. Of course this information could be used against the interests of the testing process, but it may still be worth the effort. It might also mean that parents are less likely to choose the day of the SATs for a dental appointment, or an out-of-term holiday.

39

Assessing work

Using Statements of Attainment and level descriptors from the National Curriculum to grade and assess children's work is a job most teachers have to do somewhere along the line. Often interpreting these Statements, and turning them into meaningful classroom assignments, is hard work. These tips aim to help you to do this appropriately.

1   **Stick to the Statements as they are written.** Many National Curriculum Statements appear at first sight to be vague or impenetrable, but you should avoid the temptation to read something in that is not actually there. Discuss with colleagues, mentors or others any that you are unsure about, and try to get to what is really required.

2   **Don't do it alone.** If you have a colleague in a parallel class or that you get on well with, you could try moderating one another's work. Another person's perspective, interpretation and opinion of your class's work is valuable, and gives you confidence in the quality of your own judgements. If there are no internal colleagues working at the right level, network outside your school and find people with whom you can set up mutually supportive arrangements.

3   **Use your school's portfolio of assessed work.** Many schools now have a collection of assessed work for at least the core subject areas. These portfolios show examples of work that demonstrate clear attainment at each relevant level of the National Curriculum. If your school has one, use it to compare with the work you are assessing. If it hasn't, it may be worth considering establishing one. Ask senior management for opinions and guidance on this.

4   **Use Statements of Attainment wherever possible.** The more familiar you are with the types of Statement used in national documentation, the easier it is to use them. Many of the Statements and descriptions are well-written and concise. Try using them in your planning and possibly in your feedback to children, colleagues and parents or carers.

5   **Keep in mind that your professional opinion matters.** While national documentation and school portfolios are intended to help teachers to make standardised assessments of work, your professional judgement remains paramount. Trust your judgement, and maintain a balanced view.

6   **Consult avidly your school's assessment policy.** There may be clear guidance on how work should be selected, annotated and assessed. There may be examples of the sorts of statement that are required or felt to be useful. These will be a good starting point, especially for teachers new to the job.

7   **Find out what assessing the children's work is supposed to achieve.** Sometimes it might seem that formal assessment of work is a waste of time. Different schools have different reasons for, and methods of, assessing work. Having an agreed purpose will give you a clear idea of what to include and what to leave out.

8   **Find out what will happen to the assessed outcomes.** If you know your intended audience, it is easier to decide upon what sort of language and jargon to use. Some formally assessed work may be for parental consumption, and some for specific purposes in school. Knowing who will be reading your evaluations will help you tailor your comments accordingly.

9   **If work will be sent to secondary schools into which your children feed, check what their requirements are.** Schools that will be taking your children may use the work you send them as a guide to help them stream pupils. If you know what their purpose is, it will help you decide what should and should not be included.

10 **Find out if you are looking for 'value added' information in your assessments.** 'Value added' assessment should clearly show what progress children have made. This may involve repeating the same assessment procedure, or getting children to work under exactly the same con-ditions on similar tasks at given intervals. Obviously it is important to know this so that tests and criteria are applied consistently.

40

Formal and informal assessment

Assessment can take up enormous amounts of time and effort. To make the best of opportunities for assessment, it is worth considering what exactly it is that you are trying to achieve, and what might be the least complicated and stress-free way to get what you need.

1 **Be aware that assessment's primary functions are to support and enable learning.** Without continuous assessment opportunities, you cannot know what the children have understood and what they need to learn to make progress. It is all too easy to let the assessment become an end in itself, and to forget that it is only one part of the educational process.

2 **Remember that the best assessment is often the easiest to manage.** To make realistic use of assessment it has to be manageable and consistent. Keep track of how children perform on a simple tick list and use that as your primary assessment record. Look for ways of streamlining assessment to get the maximum benefit for your efforts.

3 **It is easy to become obsessive about assessment.** If assessment is not helping you to do your job better, then it can be a waste of time. Assessment is something you will always have to do, so try to devote time and effort in proportion to the potential benefits to be gained by everyone through the process.

4 **Try to make formal assessment tasks valuable.** Of course they are important in terms of the assessment requirements laid upon you, but try to make them valuable from the children's point of view too. If the task is worthwhile in terms of learning it is more likely to be worthwhile in terms of assessment.

5   **Make sure that any formal assessments you undertake are really necessary.** If you know that they are going to serve your purpose, then go for it. If you are doing them only because you have to, check the school's documentation or discuss with management before putting yourself through it all.

6   **Try to keep assessment tasks as stress free as possible.** This is important from your point of view and from the children's. A task that is too stressful for you will not be judged fairly, and one that is too stressful for the children will not reflect their true ability. Don't work children up into a frenzy of nerves by over-stressing the importance of formal tests.

7   **Try to keep the format of assessment tasks you design familiar.** If you have to spend a lot of time preparing children for a task because it is presented in a way that they find hard to understand, then it may be more a test of their ability to understand the task, not the concept. Keeping the presentation, style and apparent purpose familiar will help to avoid this problem, by helping children to feel comfortable about what they are doing.

8   **Try to manage assessment tasks as straightforwardly as possible.** Formal assessment will often seem to be a slightly alien way of working with children. Even very young children seem to be able to understand when you explain to them what will be different and why. If they feel they know what is going on, they are more likely to undertake what is required of them without fuss.

9   **Keep notes whilst hearing children read.** This may be the best reading assessment evidence that you can gather, because it can capture significant detail, give examples, give a snapshot of skills and abilities and give a clearer indication of progress. You are also more likely to get an accurate view of children's abilities when they are in a less formal situation.

10 **Break down level descriptions into easily identifiable targets.** For instance 'mainly demarcated by capital letters and full stops' might be quantified as an average of two in every three sentences demarcated this way. Work on defining these descriptors as a school if possible, to achieve consensus. If your school has a portfolio of achievement, use this as a point of reference against which you can check your decisions.

41

Evidence of achievement

Over a period of time a body of evidence may be collected that records and demonstrates a child's ability and attainment across all or important parts of the curriculum. The best person to collect such information is the teacher. In order to make the collection of evidence a beneficial and efficient use of your time, we offer some guidelines on how to do it well.

1   **Have an eye or ear out for evidence all the time.** One way of collecting evidence of a child's best work or highest achievement is to make the collection of such work an ongoing process. It is difficult in a busy classroom but, with practice, can become part of the way you work day to day.

2   **Try putting some of the responsibility on to the children.** Especially with older children, the collection and selection of examples of their best work could become an interesting activity, perhaps towards the end of each term. You can also ask children to help each other to choose work that shows the best that they can do.

3   **Common tasks could be used for all the class at given points in the year.** While collecting evidence this way may not always gather examples of a child's full potential, it will provide a consistent and continuous body of evidence. It also means that you have samples of work from every child, as a basis for individual evidence collections.

4   **Include your own comments and observations.** A piece of work on its own might not tell the whole story. By adding notes about how the children tackled the exercise, and how much help they sought, resources they used, you can give a more complete picture. Try to keep such notes concise; you do not want to make extra work if you do not have to, and you are more likely to refer later to brief, pithy comments, rather than to extended pieces of prose.

5   **Include information about aspects of attainment that have been demon-strated.** If a piece of work has been assessed against formal criteria and will be used as evidence, it is a good idea to note which aspects of a given level descriptor have been shown to have been attained through that piece of work.

6   **Consider carefully the purpose for which evidence will be used before gathering additional evidence.** If there is no requirement that you collect evidence of attainment, you need to decide what purposes it will serve before you start collecting it. The effort expended may not be paid back. Look for guidance in school documentation and from management.

7   **Remember that your everyday documentation is good evidence.** If your planning and recording show what work children have undertaken, and perhaps an idea of their performance, then that is first rate evidence, which you may not need to supplement further.

8   **Consider other ways of gathering evidence.** Many aspects of the curriculum are hard to collect evidence for. A record of your observations or opinions is usually sufficient, but you might also want to try using photography, video, art work or tape recordings too, to add diversity and breadth to your evidence.

9   **Put the date on everything.** Try to get into the habit of putting the date on all work, and most especially on work that will be used as evidence. Having a file full of evidence is fairly useless unless it can be viewed chronologically, as you cannot track progression meaningfully without timescales.

10   **Make sure you know what the evidence will be used for in your school.** It may be that your school only requires work to demonstrate ability and not to map progress. If this is the case, then a large body of work accumulated over a period of time might not be necessary. Perhaps only one or two examples of good work are needed or perhaps work needs to be kept to serve several purposes. Find out before you give yourself additional work.

11   **Never show parents other children's evidence.** It is tempting to use one child's work as an exemplar to illuminate your comments, but this is hardly fair. You could, instead, use your school portfolio of assessed work where work is (or should be) anonymous.

42

Marking work and giving feedback

How you respond to children's work is an important aspect of communication between you and your class. It establishes expectations, emphasises targets, praises and encourages achievement, supports and extends children's work, and has a profound effect on how they feel about it, and so is worthy of careful consideration. These tips are designed to help you to make the most of feedback to foster learning.

1   **Consider what form of response is most appropriate.** Writing detailed comments on a piece of work in a reception class will not help the child concerned all that much, although might still be appropriate as a reference for an adult with an interest in what has gone on. With younger or less-able children, oral feedback directly to the child will clearly be more appropriate than written remarks. More detailed comments in Year Six can clearly serve an important role.

2   **Don't be afraid to make critical comments.** Many people feel duty bound to make only positive comments, but if a piece of work is not up to scratch the child will not learn from it unless you point out the shortcomings. However, use tact and diplomacy to avoid making your comments come across as destructive. Honesty without cruelty is the key.

3   **Try to end on a positive or encouraging note.** If you have found it necessary to make a negative response to a piece of work, a simple comment indicating that the child is capable of doing better gives the child somewhere to go, and a safety net for dignity.

4   **Give oral feedback whenever possible.** For younger children, oral feedback is essential, whereas with older children work may be commented upon in writing after school. Nevertheless, if you can find time to offer oral feedback to children of any age at some point, especially if it is positive or related to an important issue, this is likely to have more impact than a written message.

5   **Keep written feedback concise.** If written feedback is too long, it may be disregarded, and not serve the purposes for which it was intended. Try to pick out one issue, one strength and give a brief general comment about them. It is better to focus on relatively few issues, than to overwhelm children with too much.

6   **Date the work as you mark it.** Having the date on every piece of work is useful, especially if your children work on loose-leaf paper a lot. It also helps you to keep track of children's progression, when you compare work over a period of time.

7   **Consider whether words are enough!** Children get a real buzz out of showing others how well they have done, and nothing counts like the approval of somebody new. For a real pat on the back try showing the rest of the class, send them to another teacher, the head, even to assembly or a 'show and tell' session. If your school has a system of points or assertive discipline, use it because it only works when everyone contributes.

8   **Use examples of good work as an example for everyone.** If a piece of work demonstrates the qualities you are looking for, discuss it with the rest of the class. Encourage them to think about why it looks nice, what makes it clear, well structured, neatly presented and so on. Let them learn more about what is expected of them, by showing them the standards that can be achieved.

9   **Display work that you feel demonstrates significant achievement.** Even if you were not planning a display for that work, having a display that is simply for good work may provide a good incentive.

10   **When marking work, keep a focus on the intended learning outcomes.** Use them as your criteria for making evaluations. On the whole, the intended learning outcome of the task you are marking will give you a focus for your comments about the completed work. These comments will also act as a record of what the child was supposed to be focusing on for future reference.

43

Self-assessment

Encouraging children to think about their work, and reflect upon how they could do better are widely regarded as being good practice. This isn't just a matter of letting children mark themselves, but a way of helping children to make realistic evaluations of their own achievements. It can be a powerful way of building children's self-esteem, and of motivating them to work. However, some children find it difficult, so managing the situation takes some thought and some preparation. These tips are designed to help you get the children involved in their own assessment.

1   **Start to train children as soon as possible.** Children can find it very difficult to reflect on their own work. Starting the process while they are young may seem to have limited immediate benefit, but the ability to critique one's own work is a difficult skill to develop and this takes time.

2   **Get a progressive format for self-assessment.** To help children reflect in any kind of detail, work sheets that act as a guide or prompt may help. The form these sheets take could remain similar across the whole school, increasing in detail and complexity as their familiarity with the tasks and their overall abilities improve.

3   **Avoid regurgitation of your assessment of work.** Given the chance, children will simply repeat in their own words what you say in your responses to their work. To avoid this, you could simply ask them to select a piece of their work they are proud of and get them to explain why they think they did well and what they like about it.

4   **Scribe for younger or less able children.** To get any sort of relevant detail in self-assessment, you may have to act as scribe for younger children. While it would be nice to write down their comments verbatim, you may find you have to précis what they say to keep it manageable. You may also be able to use support staff or classroom volunteers to assist with the scribing.

5   **Consider how creative written work may give insight into children's ideas about themselves.** A piece of work entitled 'Why I like to be me', 'A list of ten things I am good at', or 'The best day of my life" and so on, could provide a wonderful task, but also act as a valuable self-assessment tool. Be aware, however, that some children with low self-esteem might find the task very frightening.

6   **Try to strike a balance between positive and negative reflections.** While you will naturally want to get the children to focus on positive things about themselves and their work, it is important to get them to think about what they would like to do better, or how they could improve on aspects of their work. This awareness of where they need to develop can help them set realistic goals for achievement.

7   **Reflect on what children have learned at the end of a topic.** Sometimes children move quickly from one topic to another without noticing the transition. At the end of a short topic, you could get them to think about what they have learned, what they enjoyed and perhaps what they did not like doing too. This can give a defined ending to the topic as well as providing good personal assessment evidence.

8   **Review work with the children.** When looking back at a piece or a body of work, it might be a good idea to discuss the responses the children have made with them. You could add comments that reinforce and extend the children's own thoughts. This is likely to provide opportunities for genuine dialogue and insights into children's values of themselves.

9   **Consider how and where self-assessed work will be stored.** You may want to build up a file of work that each child is proud of. What will it be? Who will have ownership of it? Who decides what goes in and what doesn't? Where and how will it be stored? How can you ensure that it is available for reference when needed (which may not be the case if it goes home)?

10   **Allow time for children to look back over their achievements.** One of the nicest things about collecting work the children are proud of is watching their reactions to it a little further down the line. Giving them access to such work is a rewarding experience for them as well as for you.

44

Assessing children with special needs

Children may come into your class already identified as having special educational needs or may, for any number of reasons, become cause for concern while in your class. You need to work with your Special Educational Needs Coordinator or support services teacher to get the best professional advice and support available. However , the chances are that it will be your responsibility to handle much of the work for assessing them initially, maintaining paper work, preparing and delivering individual education programmes and so on. UK state schools have specific procedures to follow, and this section applies primarily to these. (See also 'Working with outside agencies' in Chapter 6.)

1 **Be alert to children's needs and potential problems.** Being responsible for the initial identification of children who might have special educational needs is a daunting and rather frightening matter. Whether you are a nursery teacher or in Year Six, it is important to be alert to potential problems.

2 **Be aware of both ends of the ability spectrum.** You need to be on the look out for those very bright, but possibly bored children who may need to be stretched, as well as for those who might be struggling and might need extra support to keep up.

3 **Look out for any worrying behaviour.** Bad behaviour is sometimes a result of boredom and under-stimulation or of an inability to cope with the work being given. As well as dealing with the behaviour, consider what might be the underlying causes of it.

4 **Listen carefully.** Language skills, both expressive and receptive, can be a good indication of a child's real understanding of what is going on around them. If you become concerned about a child's ability to use language, it is a good indicator that you might need to seek extra help.

5   **Don't go it alone.** If you don't feel confident about identifying children, consult your Special Educational Needs coordinator, who will help you with the kinds of points and issues you need to put in your 'Initial Concern' paperwork. You can also talk to others in the school, who may have more experience than you of special educational needs, or who may be familiar with the child causing you concern.

6   **Use published assessment tasks.** There are many tests available which can highlight particular strengths or weaknesses, such as auditory memory, visual memory, expressive language, receptive language, hand-eye coordination and so on. Once an area of difficulty has been specifically identified, it will help you to fill in the appropriate level of paperwork, and seek the right kind of help.

7   **Use the correct terminology.** When completing the necessary forms, keep your points short, tightly observed and cover only the main areas of concern. Nevertheless, make sure that the vocabulary you use is precise, and explains explicitly what you are worried about.

8   **When writing descriptors to help you define special educational needs, make them short-term and specific.** When filling in your individual education programmes, you must be clear in your targets 'will be able to use prepositions accurately' is rather woolly and unfocused. Try instead 'will be able to use: in, on and under in a consistent and accurate manner'. This makes assessment and progress much easier to measure and record.

9   **Keep parents or carers informed.** Once you have filled in an 'Initial Concern' form, you have to record whether you have had any contact with the parents or carers on this matter or not. Although it is not a legal requirement at this stage, it may be better to let parents or carers know, at an early stage, what your concerns are and what could be done about them. This is better than risking them feeling marginalised later.

10   **Be over-cautious.** If you are not sure, but think there may be a problem, even if you think it might sort itself out, fill in the paperwork and register your concern. It is better to be safe than to let a potential problem rumble on indefinitely.

45

Differentiation

With large, mixed ability classes, delivering an effective curriculum is not possible without differentiation of tasks and the outcomes that children are expected to achieve. It is a tricky balancing act to match work to ability, in order to ensure that children are working at a level that they can cope with, but that also stretches them. Nevertheless, teachers need to be able to do this, to ensure that every child has a good chance to learn and develop.

1   **Be realistic about how much differentiation is manageable.** In most situations, catering for three groups, higher, average and lower attainers is about as much as can be achieved. This may not be perfect, but it will avoid getting bound up too often in the needs of small groups or even individuals.

2   **Differentiate the activity, not the learning outcome.** In many cases it is possible to tackle the same goal at three different levels. Although this is not always achievable, do it when you can, because it means you can discuss concepts as a class but tailor actual tasks to meet the children's individual needs, and it helps keep planning simple. It also helps less able children to avoid feeling marginalised to the same extent.

3   **Keep your assessment tasks differentiated.** If you set differentiated work it makes sense to use differentiated assessments too. Making assessment tasks fit the ways the children are able to work independently may initially make more work for you, but it will make for a more effective assessment for the children.

4   **Use different groupings for different subjects**. Someone who is below average in language may be above average in maths. It is not always possible to group children in several different ways at different times in the day, but where it is, using different groupings will allow you to cater better for individual needs.

5   **Be prepared to change groupings.** Rates of progress differ and it may become apparent that some children are either racing ahead or getting left behind. Changing their groups will help them cope better. It might also be prudent to change groupings if behaviour gets out of hand, or if you are concerned about the effect that one child is having on another.

6   **Challenge children.** It is clearly important to stretch children to prevent them from getting bored. Knowing how much stretching they can take is very difficult, but setting them a challenge, one that you think only the most able will achieve, can be a good way of finding out how well individual children can cope and persevere. Try it as a class activity and share ideas and possible solutions.

7   **Try not to let a lack of basic skills hold children back in other ways.** A child may have poor pencil control or be unable to read without support, but these things do not indicate a lack of ability in other areas. As far as possible, try to support those aspects of the work with which they struggle, but stretch them in other aspects of the curriculum.

8   **When putting children into groups, draw up a set of criteria for group formation.** How you decide upon who goes where, and who works with who can be tricky. Having a set of criteria can help take some of the guess work out of the process, but be aware that sticking rigidly to criteria can make life more complicated and may not give you the result that you intend.

9   **Differentiate whole class teaching.** One of the appealing things about whole class teaching for some is that everyone is doing the same thing at the same time. This style of teaching can still incorporate differentiated elements. Even if it is simply the expected outcome that is differentiated, as long as these expectations are recorded, it is still a valuable way of enabling children to work at levels at which they can succeed.

10 **Differentiate the support you offer.** Another way of using similar activities, but still ensuring that they are tailored to meet different children's needs, is to differentiate the level of support that they will have in order to complete the task. Be careful, however, that children who don't need support don't feel ignored.

Chapter 6   Your Professional Life

There is a great deal more to being a teacher than just teaching. Every teacher will be faced with an array of additional duties that, in time, will become second nature. However, early in a career they can cause quite a strain, not least because nobody seems to have thought to tell you what is involved until it's too late! Forewarned is at least partially forearmed.

46

Inspection

Many teachers find the idea of having someone else in the classroom, watching over their teaching, a daunting prospect. Nevertheless, such visits are part of the professional life of every teacher nowadays. However, such occasions do not have to be traumatic. If you prepare well you can make the experience less stressful and more useful. These tips are designed to help you to make inspection as positive an experience as possible.

1   **Recognise that it is worth spending time preparing**. It is all too easy to be so busy with everyday matters that it's tempting to take the attitude 'They'll have to take us as they find us'. Taking the time to make sure that you are ready for the visit will pay off in terms of your own confidence.

2   **Prepare well in advance**. It is never too early to start preparing. Get an action plan, including target dates, and take responsibility for the things that you think that you can manage. Avoid the 'groundrush' effect, where as in parachuting, everything seems to speed up horribly towards the end.

3   **Prepare for an inspection, even if one is not actually imminent.** If you work day to day towards narrowing the gap between where you are and where you think you need to be, the anxiety of the actual date should diminish. The more good record keeping and good professional practice is a matter of routine, the less stressful an inspection visit will be.

4   **Let everyone know.** Coping well with an inspection needs to be a team effort. Don't make the mistake of assuming that everyone, including cleaners, caretakers and non-teaching staff know about it. Tell them and help them to feel part of it all. After all, everyone will have an important part to play in building a good impression of the school.

5   **Talk about it.** Discussion about worries or concerns that you may have with other professionals will probably lighten the load, just because you have got them off your chest. You may even discover that there is a lot you can help one another with.

6   **Make full use of other people who have done it before.** You may well know other teachers who have been visited, or even people who are trained inspectors. Use their experience and pick their brains because they may well have some good advice, examples that you could borrow and adapt or encouraging words: it all helps!

7   **Avoid complacency based on previous successes.** Even if you or your school has had a successful inspection on an earlier occasion, do not make the mistake of assuming that the next one will be equally positive. The goal posts may well have been moved, and certainly it will involve different people with different perspectives. Treat each inspection as a new occasion to demonstrate your approach to teaching.

8   **Avoid despair based on previous negative experiences.** Even if you have had an inspection or pre-inspection that was traumatic, it doesn't mean that the next one will be. Because things change, and you have been busy, you may not have had the chance to reflect upon how much progress you have really made. Additionally, if you have seriously addressed the comments made in a previous, less successful visit, you will have plenty of evidence to demonstrate commitment to improve.

9   **Get team spirit going**. When colleagues get together and work as a team, they create a positive attitude and a favourable impression, rather than conflicting attitudes or approaches. When everyone pulls together, preparing for inspection can be a positive team-building experience.

10 **Don't get it out of proportion.** Lengthy meetings in preparation for a visit often end up being unproductive and negative. It is better to have frequent, short meetings with tight agendas and specific goals. Strong leadership doesn't hurt either so be prepared to take the bull by the horns, if your role requires it. Or be prepared to knuckle down, and really work for the sake of the school, if you are asked to do so.

11 **Make distinctions between what is urgent and what is important.** Not everything that is important is urgent and vice versa. Decide upon what is important and then try to work out which of these important things is urgent. Then you can concentrate on your highest priorities to get ready for inspection.

12 **You cannot solve every problem overnight.** It may be more sensible to make an action plan to tackle a problem you have identified, than to implement a hasty solution immediately. Often inspection looks more favourably on a considered and measured response that is still being implemented, than on a rush job or a cover up.

47

Appraisal

Appraisal is an established part of school and personal development in teaching professions, although sometimes accepted simply because it is inevitable. The aim is to help you as a teacher, and to help the school as a whole. Approach it confidently and positively, using it as a chance to evaluate your own performance, with support, to look forward to developmental opportunities, and to review where you need to go next.

1   **Have confidence.** The first and most important thing to remember is that appraisal is designed to help you perform more effectively as a teacher, and give your best to the job. If you find it intimidating, take time to discuss this with your appraiser. Good ones will take your concerns seriously, and address them as part of their negotiation with you.

2   **Take the opportunity to discuss the focus of the appraisal before you start.** You should aim to have the opportunity to plan what your appraiser should focus on in your appraisal in advance. Try to make sure that you talk to your appraiser in advance of the appraisal, to set an agenda that suits you both. If your appraiser does not raise the subject with you, you may need to tackle the subject yourself.

3   **All feedback is potentially useful**. Without impartial feedback, getting better at your job is very difficult. Appraisal aims to make impartial advice and constructive criticism available to all teachers, so try to make it an occasion to listen, take what is said on board, and move towards positive development.

4   **Be prepared to receive positive feedback.** Do not be embarrassed about receiving praise but listen carefully. Knowing what your strengths are can help you to capitalise on them and, as such, is a vital aspect of appraisal. Don't dismiss or underplay what is said to you, take it at face value.

5   **Be prepared to receive negative feedback.** What you at first hear as criticism can actually be valuable feedback. It is difficult for an appraiser to say things that they know you do not want to hear, which makes the fact that they felt it important all the more pressing. Knowing where your weaknesses are is as important as having confidence in your strengths. Don't let natural reactions to the less positive things you hear stop you from using this feedback to build plans for future improvements to your teaching.

6   **Be prepared to try to elicit feedback.** If an agenda for your appraisal has been set and comments, one way or another, are not forthcoming, be prepared to press your appraiser on these points. It's not a bad idea to have prepared in advance some specific questions you would like answered about your teaching.

7   **Use the feedback to set yourself targets.** Take the opportunity to discuss potential ways forward and, in conjunction with your appraiser, set yourself targets or suggested routes for tackling issues.

8   **Take reassurance from the fact that all appraisal is confidential.** The advice and feedback given to you will not become common currency in the staff room, unless you choose that it should.

9   **Look for developmental opportunities.** The appraisal is often your best opportunity to discuss what you feel are your professional training needs, in order to help you to do your job better. Appraisal is designed to look forward as well as backwards. Consider, for example, how you can use chances to observe others teach, as an opportunity for your own personal development.

10 **Remember that everyone is in the same boat.** Everyone in your school should be the subject of appraisal, from headteachers to Newly Qualified Teachers, so there is no reason to feel that you are under special scrutiny or that you are being treated differently to other members of staff.

11 **Remember that appraisal is your right.** It is a means of letting you know that what you do is of value, as well as highlighting areas of future development.

48

Mentoring and supporting student teachers

The chances are that at some point in your career you will be asked to support other people's professional development. With more and more of a student teacher's time being spent in school, and the increasing use of mentoring in the continuation of the learning process for Newly Qualified Teachers, this role is more likely than ever to be part of your professional duties.

1 **Get as much information about your students as possible, in advance.** Universities and colleges might not be very forthcoming with information about the students, how they have performed on the course so far, and any issues that might be useful to know about in advance. Try to get to talk to the student's tutor before the practice begins.

2 **Be prepared to give practical demonstrations.** Learning the tricks of managing a classroom takes time, and students and Newly Qualified Teachers might need to watch you in action in order to be able to develop or reflect upon these skills for themselves. If possible, give them a running commentary; they may not otherwise notice some of the things you do automatically.

3 **Start students off with non-threatening situations.** Give them the chance to get involved in simple activities that they can plan and manage for themselves, such as reading a story or focusing on an aspect of small group work. This will help give them the confidence they need before tackling bigger things.

4 **Let them know what you will be looking for**. There will be times when you will have to make formal observations of students and possibly Newly Qualified Teachers. Let them know what you will be focusing on and what you will be looking for in advance, so they have the best possible chance of achieving your expectations.

5   **Encourage students and Newly Qualified Teachers to observe different teachers.** Any opportunities for picking up ideas about teaching and managing a classroom, in as many different contexts as possible, can only be good. It will also take some of the pressure away from you.

6   **Let the students evaluate their performance first.** If students can identify good and bad points in their teaching, then 90% of the work is done already. You may still need to highlight points they have missed, but letting them come up with the majority of the issues makes for a more comfortable experience for both of you. Be aware that they are likely to be extremely self-critical at first.

7   **Plan together.** If you leave sole responsibility for planning to students, then problems that could have been identified, solved, and avoided at the planning stage, may surface in the classroom, having detrimental effects on their teaching and their confidence and on your class. Joint planning also provides opportunities for students to understand the mechanics of how you go about preparing for classroom activities.

8   **Be prepared to let them make mistakes.** It is tempting to quietly intervene when you spot early-warning signs of potential problems that your student has missed. Identifying and tackling one's own mistakes is a valuable learning experience for students. If you intervene, they will not see, for example, the consequences of allowing minor disruptions to go unchallenged. Obviously, if something is seriously going wrong, don't just leave them to suffer the consequences; intervene with tact and diplomacy.

9   **Remember that students need encouragement and reassurance.** Sometimes they need more than the children themselves. It is difficult and stressful being put in the position of doing an experienced person's job while that person watches you. Help them to remember that you went through the process yourself when you were being trained.

10   **Make sure that you don't over-commit yourself to other tasks.** Someone might be taking responsibility for your class for eight weeks, but that does not mean you are going to be free to get on with all those jobs that have stacked up over the term. In fact you may be amazed by how little free time you get by being out of the classroom while a student is with your children.

11 **Prepare for a failing student.** If you feel that a student or Newly Qualified Teacher is not coping, hard though it is, it will be your responsibility to broach this with them. Discuss your concerns with university tutors, your headteacher, and the students themselves. Try to come up with strategies for dealing with the situation, setting small, manageable targets and monitoring them daily, taking back overall responsibility for the class, arranging for additional auxiliary support for a short while or whatever.

12 **Remember that mentoring can be a rewarding experience for you as well.** It can give you opportunities to focus on your own teaching styles; it will make you think more carefully about what you do and why you do it. Though it can be hard work, the benefits should outweigh the drawbacks.

49

Being a Newly Qualified Teacher

As a Newly Qualified Teacher you may feel swamped with information, bewildered by all the frantic comings and going, left out, or perhaps the butt of the jokes and the banter, and terrified of the prospect of flying without a co-pilot. Here are some things that you can do before you start, and in the early days and weeks, that might help you find your feet.

1   **Aim to visit the school if you can, when it is in session, before you start.** Nothing can prepare you better than looking around your new school while it is in full swing. Having a feel for the place, its routines, its layout and the people that are in it before you start is a real confidence booster. If at all possible, once you are appointed, get in before the holidays start.

2   **Try to get hold of useful information about your school.** This is likely to include copies of the school prospectus, staff lists, a map of the building, a timetable, the sorts of information that the parents or carers will be receiving and asking questions about, and how the register should be filled in. Get anything that you think might come in handy, and spend some time perusing it, so you know the right kinds of questions to ask before you start to teach.

3   **Get hold of copies of school policy documentation and schemes of work.** Many of the policies will not appear to be instantly relevant; ignore them for the time being but file them for later reference. With those that will affect the way you work from the first day, take the time to read them before term starts, and look at how they will impact on your day-to-day life.

4   **Check discipline strategies.** Knowing the range of sanctions available to you is important for your own confidence, as well as for managing the behaviour of your new class. If you can achieve consistency from day one, then so much the better.

5   **Read Assessment, Marking and Recording policies.** This will give you a good insight into the kinds of areas that you may need to ask about, and will help you keep appropriate records up to date right from the outset.

6   **Gather pupil records.** It helps if you are familiar with the names of the children in your class, and have an idea of their personalities. Be careful not to label children though, as they tend to live up to expectations. Keep a healthy scepticism about what you are told about pupils: some views you hear may be jaundiced!

7   **Ensure that your lesson plans are well prepared.** This will give you confidence. Also prepare teaching materials well in advance. Most new teachers prepare far too much material at first, but it is better to have too much than too little. You will also normally be able to use any surplus later.

8   **Be ready to ask colleagues for help.** You will probably be assigned a mentor. You should use this person to good effect. In the unlikely event of you using too much of their time, they will let you know. Make use also of informal mentors, and others who are close enough to newly qualified status to remember what it is like to be just starting out.

9   **Take opportunities for support.** You may be offered training to extend your skills early on, and you will probably be offered opportunities to meet with fellow Newly Qualified Teachers from elsewhere. Go along, it is good to exchange stories of disaster and success. You will find that everyone is in the same boat, and that you can learn a lot from each other.

10   **Be prepared to be observed.** Your headteacher or mentor will almost certainly want to observe your teaching from time to time. The areas they will want to look at will probably include class management, relevant subject expertise, appropriate teaching skills and styles, use of resources, your understanding of the needs of the pupils, and your ability to establish appropriate relationships with both pupils and colleagues.

11   **Keep a sense of humour.** It is not worth dwelling for long on lessons that don't go as well as you would wish. You must not expect to get it right straight away. Try not to take every minor setback to heart. Use each seeming disaster as a learning opportunity.

12   **Eat and sleep well.** You will probably spend most of your first term feeling exhausted. Avoid taking on anything more than you absolutely have to. It is important not to get too tired.

13   **Be prepared for minor illnesses.** Many new teachers find they pick up every germ going around a school, so stock up in advance with cold remedies, throat sweets, and perhaps even treatments for head lice.

14   **Give yourself time to relax at home.** Avoid talking about school all the time in your leisure hours; you need time away. Try to keep a proper balance between being well enough prepared to be comfortable in your work, and having some chances to forget all about school for a while.

15   **Arrive with plenty of time to spare.** Finding resources and setting up can take longer than you might think. It is worth getting out of bed an hour earlier than you might otherwise have done, so that if travel arrangements go wrong, you still have some leeway.

16   **Take a classroom survival kit.** Having a supply, for example, of erasers, pencil sharpeners, a staple gun and staples, coloured biros, a whistle and a craft knife could all help save your neck on the first day.

17   **Put together a personal survival kit.** You may need spare clothes in case of spills and messy accidents, for example. In many staff rooms you will be more welcome if you bring your own mug on the first day, and a small supply of tea and coffee, until you suss out the coffee fund. Many teachers also like a personal stereo and a tape of calming music for the times when the children are out of the class, and preparation or tidying-up work needs to be done.

18   **Don't try to reorganise everything on your first day.** You will have a lot to cope with in the early weeks, so it might be as well to live with your classroom as it is at first, until you and the children have a chance to settle down.

19   **Make friends with the non-teaching staff.** They are often your best allies. The nursery nurses, auxiliary, cleaners and caretaker, the dinner ladies and kitchen staff can be great resources and support. You may get useful information about the children (and about other staff) from them too.

20   **Keep a journal of your first year of teaching.** In this you can record what went well, and not so well, and this will help you to plan and prepare for the subsequent year. It's also helpful in preparing for your first appraisal, and can provide terrific reading to look back on when you are an old hand at the job.

50

Working with outside agencies

As a teacher you will probably need to liaise with a growing number of outside agencies. These might include doctors, nurses, social workers, members of the Police Force, educational psychologists, speech therapists, university and college staff, family support units, multicultural support workers, educational support services staff and colleagues from other schools. These tips aim to help you to develop a fully professional approach to working with any of these people.

1   **Check school procedures when dealing with external agencies.** There may be clearly defined steps that you need to follow, for a variety of different issues. It is important that you are aware of these, and abide by the guidelines that are set down for inter-agency interaction.

2   **Find out what your responsibilities are.** Are you the best person to make contact with outside agencies? Is it your responsibility to make the first approach? Who else from the school needs to be involved? Where does your responsibility start and finish?

3   **Find out whose job it is to keep everyone else informed**. When working on a particular case, it is important to find this out because it may be your responsibility, or that of your special educational needs coordinator, or that of the school's administrative assistant or even that of the headteacher.

4   **Keep individual records up to date.** When liaising with any outside agencies, it is vital to have accurate and up-to-date information on the child in question. This will enable the child to get the best support possible, and you will be above reproach in your dealings. You may need to fill in and maintain special reports or documentation. These will be important in most procedures that involve outside agencies.

5   **Keep notes about any communication.** If you talk on the phone, keep a record of dates, times, content, contact name and so on. These notes and any other correspondence should be kept with the rest of the case notes. Don't try to rely on your memory. Your life is much too busy to remember all the details you may need.

6   **Be prepared to express your opinions.** If called to a meeting about a child, you will almost certainly be asked to give your professional opinion, as you spend proportionally more time with the child than any other professional. Rely on your records and stick to what you *know* to be true. Try to back assertions with evidence of some kind, for example, notes from incidents, which illustrate the problem as you see it.

7   **Be ready to speak in front of parents or carers.** What you are going to say, or need to say, may not be what the parents want to hear, for a variety of reasons. It is part of your job to say what is necessary, however hard this may seem. Stick to facts and try to support them with evidence, dates and so on. At the same time, remember how painful this is likely to be for the parents or carers, and use all of your tact and diplomacy.

8   **Keep a case diary.** Any relevant incidents or occurrences should be noted carefully. It is amazing how fast you forget the details of incidents, particularly if they are unpleasant, as you may wish to put them out of your mind.

9   **Get support from your colleagues.** Your mentor (if you have one), special educational needs cooordinator, and headteacher should all be able to give you advice about who to talk to and when to do it. Especially if you are new to the job, don't feel that you need to tackle everything yourself.

10   **Don't take it all home with you.** It is very difficult when you care about the children you teach, not to continue to worry about them outside the teaching situation. It is natural to be concerned, but once you have done everything that you can in identifying problems, seeking specialist support, and pressing for appropriate action to take, try not to let such problems take over your life. You will be better able to look after the children in your care if you also look after yourself.

51

Liaising with parents or carers

An aspect of teaching that is difficult to get used to, and impossible to predict, is liaising with parents or carers. They may seek your advice, press you for information, confront you, perhaps even cry on your shoulder, and most of it will not wait until open night, so be prepared! Even experienced teachers often find working with parents a complex part of the job, so these tips are designed to prepare the ground for it.

1   **Remember that most parents or carers are on your side.** Most of the time, most parents realise what a difficult job teaching is, and that their child may be far from an angel. Most parents will be happy to cooperate with what you suggest, as they know you have the interests of their child at heart.

2   **Prepare in advance for open night.** Making notes that are specific and accurate to each child can help jog your memory. Have work to hand that may demonstrate the main points. If you have a lot of children, it can help to have an annotated class photograph to help you to make sure that you are talking about the right child, especially if several children share the same first name.

3   **Remember that some parents find speaking to teachers a real trial.** Especially those who have had unhappy experiences of school themselves, as parents often find the whole atmosphere of school traumatic. Even parents who did well at school themselves can find parents' evenings nerve-racking experiences.

4   **Don't forget that although you teach lots of children, parents are only really interested in their own.** Parents can be concerned to the point of obsession about their own children, and are often hungry for information about what goes on in school.

5   **Avoid making comparisons between children to parents.** You should focus on the child under discussion, rather than their best friends, or the brightest child in the class, or a sibling. In this context particularly, comparisons are odious.

6   **Focus on behaviour rather than on personality.** Parents are likely to be receptive to requests to help change behaviour, but may feel threatened if you concentrate on personality. They may feel you are being very critical of them; after all, personality types often run in families.

7   **Have a system to prevent some parents taking up all the time you have.** Concerned parents are very time-consuming, and it may be difficult to bring an interview to an end. Try timed appointments at parents' evenings, (even though they always tend to over-run). If you are seeing individual parents out of school time in the classroom, you may sometimes need to arrange for a colleague to 'interrupt' you after a suitable time, say 20 minutes.

8   **If you are confronted by an angry or upset parent, remain calm.** Listen to what they have to say, and give them time to get it off their chests. Often aggression is related to fear, and the parent may be upset and worried about what you will do or say. Try to get to the root of the problem, it may well be something that is easy to sort out. In any case, you need to get a clear picture of what is the central issue.

9   **Don't let yourself be intimidated.** If a parent wants to talk to you in an inappropriate manner, or at an inappropriate time, or about something inappropriate, don't let them. Try to arrange an appointment with a more suitable person or at a more suitable time. However, do not ignore the problem, as that could make matters worse. If offering to arrange an appointment does not work, try to send for help, preferably from a member of senior management.

10 **Have any relevant data written down.** If you do have to confront unhelpful parents or carers with news of bad behaviour or poor work, have something concrete in front of you, as a basis for discussion. You might be surprised what a calming effect irrefutable evidence can have.

11 **Avoid embarrassing parents or carers**. Many issues can be sorted out quickly at the beginning or at the end of the day. However trivial or mundane the matter may seem to you, a parent may not thank you for discussing in public problems you may be having with their child. Respect confidentiality, and you are likely to get a more cooperative response.

12   **If you suspect a meeting may become awkward, get back-up.** Have another adult in the classroom or within shouting distance. You probably won't need them but it will give valuable moral support.

13   **Be as positive as you can.** Parents or carers, like children, respond well to praise, but make sure that you also tell the truth. If you have something unpalatable to say, try to think of something good you can say at the beginning of the conversation. Ideally, end the discussion with suggestions about positive action, something concrete that you would like the child or the parent to do.

14   **Be honest.** Don't try to cover up a potential problem. Most parents or carers would rather face a problem and try to deal with it, than come to feel that you had not been totally honest with them at a later date.

15   **Check school procedures on parent–teacher interactions.** This will make sure that you are assured of the school's support if anything should go wrong, and will mean that you are confident that you are acting within the appropriate framework.

52

Looking after yourself

In your life as a primary school teacher, you have to look after yourself because nobody is going to do it for you. Teaching is an exhausting and demanding job, despite popular rumours to the contrary, but taking the time and trouble to help yourself to cope, and to manage stressful situations is time well spent. Here are some tried and tested ideas for helping to look after yourself.

1   **Remind yourself of why you started teaching.** You may have discovered that the pay isn't up to much any more, and holidays get shorter as work takes over, but there are aspects of the job that are exciting and stimulating, try to dwell on these things more, and the not-so-wonderful bits less.

2   **Be realistic about taking work home.** Few teachers can get by without taking some work home, but taking too much home is not a good idea. Try to strike a balance: only take what is essential and try to get as much as possible done before leaving school. If you can, try to keep it down to just one job a night. It just becomes depressing if you keep on taking the same tasks backwards and forwards between home and school.

3   **Try to make space for your personal development**. You will be expected to update your skills and knowledge as a teacher. Try to take opportunities for training that also give you skills that might help you to keep on top of the job too. Any form of training where you meet others is likely to help you to build important networks, which will be useful to you. It can also be a real boost to be in the company of a group of adults, since most of your life is spent with children.

4   **Be aware of your strengths and weaknesses.** Try to be realistic about yourself, take pride in your strengths and enjoy the benefits these strengths bring. Try to tackle your weaknesses but also give yourself permission to be imperfect. Just because you have a weakness it doesn't mean that you have to work three times as hard at it to keep up.

5   **Keep learning about teaching.** The more you can learn about teaching, the more tips and experience you can pick up along the way, the more efficiently you can learn to do your job. Read the 'trade papers', try to allocate time to keep up with current thinking about teaching, and use every opportunity you can to learn from people with more experience than you.

6   **Don't ignore stress.** There are no prizes for keeping going until you drop, in fact quite the reverse, so it is much better to face the fact that you are stressed and try to do something about it. If you begin to suffer from sleeplessness, weight gain or loss, eating problems, headaches, irritability or other signs of stress, try to identify the causes of your stress, and find ways to tackle them.

7   **Allow yourself to feel angry.** Anger is a common reaction to stress and is often not clearly directed at anything in particular. People often feel powerless and this makes them frustrated. It is important not to bottle anger up, but try to let it out in situations that will not simply pass your stress on to the children or on to colleagues. Exercise, do some vigorous gardening, take a long walk, buy a pet, or try smashing something that will make a satisfying noise but won't hurt you or your wallet.

8   **Have some fun.** Try to find ways to de-stress yourself by doing things that make you happy. A little hedonism goes a long way. Think about the sorts of things that you enjoy such as cooking, reading, walking in the countryside, roller blading, hang gliding, spending time with friends, moderate drinking, whatever; and make time for them. Keep on smiling. Everyone hates Mondays, but it's still a brilliant job!

9   **Don't be afraid to go to the doctor.** Severe stress can often be helped by medication in the short term. Just because there may not be any physical signs of illness does not mean that the doctor will not be able to help; at least give yourself the chance to find out if there is anything that could help.

10   **Get a life outside school.** Family and friends still need you, and you need them if you give yourself the time to think about it. Try not to neglect them, indulge yourself in your hobbies every once in a while, plan (and take) a short break or holiday. Use anything you can to help you to keep everything in perspective.

53

Coping with your workload

Many people assume that the point of being a teacher is to teach, but increasingly it seems that teaching is just one small part of your professional commitments. Once you have filled in your planning sheets, evaluations, assessments, Individual Educational Plans, arranged a meeting with Educational Support Services, updated your schemes of work, and so on, there seems to be little time left for teaching. Of course, all these things are supposed to help you do your job properly, but how do you manage to juggle all these aspects of your work effectively?

1   **Prioritise your work.** Ask yourself which of the things you need to do are urgent *and* important. Deal quickly with urgent work or materials you need for the next day, and leave record and assessment work until you have a space to fit them in. Don't ignore them, however; try to block out some time to catch up with administrative work. If you leave it all on the back boiler, this will become a cause of stress in itself.

2   **Use your administrative support staff.** Their jobs make them more likely to able to efficiently process standard paperwork, and to do typing or to copy work. Try to ensure that you don't do things you don't have to do, if someone else can.

3   **Make good use of existing learning resource materials.** There are a great many print-based resources that give children the opportunity to 'learn by doing'. Making the most of these resources may free up more of your time to spend with individuals or small groups.

4   **Manage your marking.** Try to spread heavy marking loads out evenly throughout the week. Where possible, plan when homework should be handed in, so that it does not all arrive in one lump on Monday morning. If you phase the handing-in of work, you can spread it out over a period of time, rather than rushing it all together. There are few things more daunting than a big pile of marking lurking on the corner of your desk.

5   **Keep files, not piles.** If you think how long you can spend riffling through piles of work for a particular paper, you will know in your heart that spending time organising a decent filing system is time well spent. There is also a great deal of satisfaction to be gained by establishing your own particular system that works well for you.

6   **Keep your, and everyone else's, paperwork to a minimum.** Your colleagues will be grateful if you don't add paper to their load. Keep any written documents short and clearly focused. Make explicit what should be done with these documents. You could have headers for all documentation that show where each piece of paper goes or what should be done with it.

7   **Don't carry your workload around in your head.** You can only really do one thing at a time, so try to avoid letting yourself be sidetracked. If you are teaching, teach, if you are marking, mark. Getting a job out of the way makes you feel ready to tackle the next one, whereas only half completed jobs just pile up and often never get finished. Use lists to help you to make sure that you don't forget things. Consider carrying a small notebook with you at all times, so you can jot down reminders to yourself.

8   **Photocopy whatever you can.** Do not rewrite what can be reused. This applies to planning, assessment, worksheets and so on. Nevertheless, be really careful not to infringe copyright, as this can carry heavy penalties both for you and for the school.

9   **Set specific times for specific preparation jobs.** Give yourself a set time to do a job and stick to it. If you decide that you are going to work until 10 o'clock, only work until 10 o'clock. If you only want to spend Sunday afternoon preparing for Monday morning, only spend Sunday afternoon. Try not to let work spill over into every part of your life.

10 **Make sure a job is worthwhile.** Will it be time well spent? Will it cut your workload? Is it important that this job be completed in the near future? If not, is it really necessary? You may need to be ruthless in your task management, if you are to keep on top of your work.

54

Being an effective colleague

Working in a school can be really miserable if the people around you are not supportive and helpful. Try to start by ensuring that the people around you find you a helpful and supportive colleague and you may be delighted at how the condition can spread.

1   **Help out when the going gets tough.** If someone in your school is struggling with a time-consuming or monotonous task, it can make a big difference if you are prepared to roll up your sleeves and lend a hand. With luck they will reciprocate when you are having a tough time too.

2   **Don't spring surprises on colleagues unnecessarily.** If you need to get colleagues to do something for you, such as make contributions to a new scheme of work, complete a curriculum audit or produce work for a display, give them plenty of time and as much guidance as you can. It may even be possible to get part of a staff meeting set aside to do the task collectively, which could save everyone's time.

3   **Keep to deadlines, especially when they have an impact on others.** If your contribution is late you may inadvertently disrupt your colleagues' plans. If it becomes apparent that you are not going to be able to meet a deadline, let others know as soon as possible. This will give them a chance to reorganise or redistribute the work.

4   **Note what your colleagues appreciate in what you do.** Try to do more of these things whenever you can! This will be wonderful for the atmosphere of the school, and will probably give you a rosy glow too.

5   **Try to be sensitive to how your colleagues are feeling.** It is easy to forget to take the trouble to pay others a little attention. You may be able to help them with a worry or problem simply by being available and aware of what is going on. A good listener is a valuable colleague, and everyone needs some help from time to time.

6 **Don't wade in where angels fear to tread.** Everyone has teaching days that they would rather forget. Support colleagues when they want support, but be ready to let them deal with things at their own pace and in their own style. If you make an offer and it is refused, withdraw gently and don't take offence. People often need to sort out things for themselves.

7 **Be considerate when sharing teaching areas.** Storage space may be limited and work space will easily become cluttered. Remember that setting up takes long enough without having to clear up other people's mess. As far as possible, negotiate in advance how space will be used, and what your joint guidelines will be.

8 **Be punctual for meetings.** Try to be on time so that others are not kept waiting. If it transpires that you are going to be late, try to send a message or inform the chair of the meeting to make a start without you. If you are the chair then try to delegate where possible. No one likes to be kept waiting, especially when everyone has a hundred-and-one jobs that need doing.

9 **Keep colleagues informed about what you are doing.** Others need to know what you are up to, what changes you might be making to displays in shared areas, or to the furniture layout. There is nothing worse than coming into a shared area to find that all has changed with no prior consultation.

10 **Leave teaching spaces as you found them or better.** If you move furniture, or use a display board or use messy resources, try to leave the room ready to be used by others. Encourage the children to clear up their own mess and to leave the space tidy.

55

Working with administrative and support staff

Non-teaching staff play an increasingly important role in the effective running of your school. Developing a cooperative and mutually considerate working relationship with your support staff and nursery nurses makes a critical contribution to your being able to cope with your workload.

1   **Never neglect the courtesies.** After all, you are both trained professionals in the classroom, bringing particular expertise and abilities to your respective work. Even if individual members of your support staff can be difficult or inflexible, you will find it useful to gain their respect and co-operation. Ask rather than instruct and offer genuine thanks for the work that they have done.

2   **Get feedback from support staff on the way that you work with them.** Get them to say which parts of the way that you work are helpful to them, and which give them cause for concern. Apart from improving the effectiveness of the relationship, it will also help you with your own self-evaluation of your performance.

3   **Encourage your nursery nurses or support staff to get together with others.** Their own professional updating and exposure to best practice is as important as your own. Information about opportunities for nursery nurses and auxiliaries is scarce, but your headteacher should be able to provide some suggestions. You can also use your own networks to put support staff in touch with others in neighbouring schools, to their mutual benefit.

4 **Describe the precise nature and priority of each task you ask them to do.** When do you need it for? How many do you need? Who else needs them? How long should it take? Don't expect your colleagues to be mind readers, who automatically know what you want. If you do, you are likely to be disappointed.

5 **Don't expect disorganisation on your part to produce furious activity on theirs.** Try to give fair notice for tasks you want them to do for you. Provide a clear statement of what you need doing. Check that they understand what is required of them, and that the task is achievable in the time you have given. Your own professional behaviour is likely to be conducive to good working relationships.

6 **Make sure that they get credit for what they do.** Praise is always a good motivator, but don't keep it private. If their contribution has been particularly good or critical to success, give your support staff public acknowledgement and credit. This pays high dividends in the long term.

7 **Treat your support staff as equal partners.** If there are cultural or status barriers between you, do what you can to try to break them down. Remember that effective team work includes everyone regardless of job description.

8 **Help them to do a decent job.** Give them all the information and paper-work that they need. The art of effective delegation is to give people responsibility for what they do, but also to provide support and inspiration to help them to do their job well. Also make sure you give them opportunities to try out their own ideas, and make a creative input into the work.

9 **Play to their strengths.** First of all, find out about the talents they bring in to the classroom. It might be that you can share tasks and play to your respective strengths and abilities. Make the most of what they can offer.

10 **Include them in training and social events.** A whole-school training session should ideally be exactly that. It is tempting to get the auxiliaries to do sorting out or tidying up tasks, while everyone else sits in a meeting or a training session, but auxiliaries and nursery nurses are responsible for the children's education too. Think carefully about how support staff can be included to best effect, however, and don't make them sit through sessions that have no relevance to them.

56

Ten things you should never do, and some home truths

Throughout this book we have endeavoured to be as positive and encouraging as possible. We all know, however, that when we start teaching there is always plenty of advice on what not to do. The following set of tips, based on the collective wisdom of teachers through the centuries, is offered tongue-in-cheek. All of them are apocryphal, and all of them are at least partially true. We follow these, and end the book, with some home truths, that may seem like clichés, but actually contain a lot of genuine wisdom.

1 **Don't fall out with the really important people.** These include: the school administrative assistant, the caretaker, the cleaner and most importantly of all, the person who holds the key to the stock cupboard. You can probably get away with falling out with just about anyone else for a short time, but if ever a rift or disagreement with any of the above should begin to show itself, you need to act fast. Offer: flowers, chocolates, tickets to the match and plenty of grovelling! You might just about get away with it.

2 **Don't pass personal comments about other members of staff in front of the children.** Such 'slips of the tongue' have an unfortunate tendency to pass from one child to another until they find their way right back to the very person who was *not* meant to hear them. Children, in their innocence, make all-too-faithful messengers.

3 **Don't be surprised by how well you can be misquoted.** Children have an incredible ability to completely misinterpret, twist and quote out of context. The stories that get back to parents about the things you have done and said could make your hair curl. Fortunately, most of the time, parents are aware of the problem – they may well have heard the gossip about the things they are supposed to have done and said that has been going around school too, so are not unsympathetic to the situation.

4   **Don't believe 90% of the tales children tell you about their parents.** Many a parent has been horrified to read about herself in her child's news books, and has been amazed to discover the ability of her child to create a whole imaginative world that she completely fails to recognise as life at home.

5   **Don't rely on the children to forget.** Children seem to have an unnerving knack of remembering all those incidents and rash promises you would rather they *did* forget and forgetting all those things that they really need to remember. Never make a rash promise you can't keep; you will be reminded of it for ever afterwards.

6   **Don't smile before Christmas.** Clearly this tip cannot be taken literally, but its essence can. It is really about maintaining an air of mystery, keeping your cards close to your chest, and keeping the children guessing until you've got their measure, and they've got yours. Perhaps it should be 'Don't smile at anyone, unless they have earned it, before Christmas'.

7   **Don't be surprised if children behave badly on windy days.** Nobody knows why this is the case, but everyone swears it is true. Be prepared for a bumpy ride on a stormy day, as children seem to get wilder the stronger the breezes blow.

8   **Never forget to be really grateful for your Christmas presents.** Children love to buy their teachers presents at Christmas. They like to choose them themselves. Frequently they are not precisely what you would choose for yourself. But look at it this way: you will never have to buy bath salts again. And you will be made very welcome at your local Oxfam shop.

9   **Never take at face value the child who says 'It wasn't me!'** Many teachers could be rich if they had a pound for every time they had heard this assertion. Take it with a pinch of salt, and investigate further before you punish the assumed culprits.

10 **Never wear white in the classroom.** You can guarantee that the day you dress in cool, pale colours, will be the day you have to mop up 'accidents', come into contact with the paint pots, and have a close encounter with the toner from the photocopier. Go for machine-washable, dark colours, with an uneven pattern, or buy shares in a dry cleaning shop.

Home truths

1   **Don't forget what it is like to be a child.** If you can dredge up such memories it will, of course, help you present your lessons in a more interesting and appropriate manner. But more importantly it will also help you to forgive. If you can remember what it was like you will also remember that, for the children, all this education business doesn't seem all that important or relevant. If you can remember that, it is much easier to cope with how impossibly frustrating children can sometimes be.

2   **Don't forget how much fun learning can be.** As a teacher it is easy to get wrapped up in how to teach, so much so that we can forget how to learn too. The children often, and unwittingly, give us so many things to think about, learn about and enjoy. Perhaps they can teach us as many things that are really important as we can teach them.

3   **Don't take it all too seriously**. There are a great many reasons to take teaching too seriously, parents, policies, pupils and politicians to name but a few, but if you do take it all too seriously it soon becomes a very stressful and unpleasant job. For your sake and the sake of the children you teach, try to relax and enjoy the good times, young children really can be the most rewarding people to work with.

4   **Remember there is always another day.** However tough the going is, and however exhausted and disheartened you may feel, it often all looks better in the morning. Try to start each day anew, leaving behind the disillusionment of the day before, and you may be amazed how much better it all appears.

Some Helpful Books

Below is a list of books we have found useful and informative over the years, and which have helped to inform our practice.

Anning, A (1991) *The First Years of School,* Open University Press, Buckingham.

Athey, C (1990) *Extending Thought in Young Children: a parent–teacher partnership,* Paul Chapman Publishing, London.

Battelheim, B and Zelan, K (1982) *On Learning to Read,* Penguin Books, Harmondsworth.

Beard, R (1987) *Developing Reading 3–13,* Hodder and Stoughton, London.

Bird, M H (1991) *Mathematics for Young Children,* Routledge, London.

Bonnett, M (1994) *Children's Thinking,* Cassell, London.

Chambers, A (1991) *The Reading Environment,* Thimble Press, Stroud, Glos.

Colwell, E (1980) *Storytelling,* Thimble Press, Stroud, Glos.

Cullingford, C (1990) *The Nature of Learning,* Cassell, London.

Donaldson, M (1987) *Children's Minds,* Fontana Press, London.

Harlen, W and Jelly, S (1991) *Developing Science in the Primary Classroom,* Oliver and Boyd, Harlow, Essex.

Harlen, W (1987) *Teaching and Learning Primary Science,* Paul Chapman Publishing, London.

Holt, J (1964) *How Children Fail,* Penguin Books, Harmondsworth.

Leibeck, P (1984) *How Children Learn Mathematics,* Penguin Books, Harmondsworth.

McGregor, R and Myers, M (1991) *Telling the Whole Story,* Acer, Australia (Victoria).

Nias, J (1989) *Primary Teachers Talking,* Routledge, London.

Pollard, A and Tann, S (1987) *Reflective Teaching in the Primary School,* Cassell, London.

Proctor, A *et al.* (1995) *Learning to Teach in the Primary Classroom,* Routledge, London.

Ralston, M V (1993) *An Exchange of Gifts,* Pippin Publishing Ltd, Ontario, Canada

Thornton, S (1995) *Children Solving Problems,* Harvard, USA.

Wells, G (1986) *The Meaning Makers,* Hodder and Stoughton, London.

Whitehead, M (1990) *Language and Literarcy in the Early Years,* Paul Chapman Publishing, London.

Index